NEW DIRECTIONS FOR EVALUATION
A Publication of the American Evaluation Association

Gary T. Henry, *Georgia State University*
EDITOR-IN-CHIEF

Jennifer C. Greene, *Cornell University*
EDITOR-IN-CHIEF

Scandinavian Perspectives on the Evaluator's Role in Informing Social Policy

Thomas A. Schwandt
Indiana University

EDITOR

Number 77, Spring 1998

JOSSEY-BASS PUBLISHERS
San Francisco

SCANDINAVIAN PERSPECTIVES ON THE EVALUATOR'S ROLE IN INFORMING
SOCIAL POLICY
Thomas A. Schwandt (ed.)
New Directions for Evaluation, no. 77
Jennifer C. Greene, Gary T. Henry, Editors-in-Chief

Microfilm copies of issues and articles are available in 16mm and 35mm,
as well as microfiche in 105mm, through University Microfilms Inc., 300
North Zeeb Road, Ann Arbor, Michigan 48106-1346.

New Directions for Evaluation is indexed in Contents Pages in Education,
Higher Education Abstracts, and Sociological Abstracts.

ISSN 1097-6736   ISBN 0-7879-9847-8

NEW DIRECTIONS FOR EVALUATION is part of The Jossey-Bass Education
Series and is published quarterly by Jossey-Bass Inc., Publishers, 350 Sansome Street, San Francisco, California 94104-1342.

SUBSCRIPTIONS cost $63.00 for individuals and $105.00 for institutions,
agencies, and libraries. Prices subject to change.

EDITORIAL CORRESPONDENCE should be addressed to the Editors-in-Chief,
Jennifer C. Greene, Department of Policy Analysis and Management, MVR
Hall, Cornell University, Ithaca, NY 14853-4401, or Gary T. Henry,
School of Policy Studies, Georgia State University, P.O. Box 4039, Atlanta,
GA 30302-4039.

www.josseybass.com

Printed in the United States of America on acid-free recycled paper containing 100 percent recovered waste paper, of which at least 20 percent is
postconsumer waste.

NEW DIRECTIONS FOR EVALUATION
Sponsored by the American Evaluation Association

EDITORIAL POLICY AND PROCEDURES

New Directions for Evaluation, a quarterly sourcebook, is an official publication of the American Evaluation Association. The journal publishes empirical, methodological, and theoretical works on all aspects of evaluation. A reflective approach to evaluation is an essential strand to be woven through every volume. The editors encourage volumes that have one of three foci: (1) craft volumes that present approaches, methods, or techniques that can be applied in evaluation practice, such as the use of templates, case studies, or survey research; (2) professional issue volumes that present issues of import for the field of evaluation, such as utilization of evaluation or locus of evaluation capacity; (3) societal issue volumes that draw out the implications of intellectual, social, or cultural developments for the field of evaluation, such as the women's movement, communitarianism, or multiculturalism. A wide range of substantive domains is appropriate for *New Directions for Evaluation;* however, the domains must be of interest to a large audience within the field of evaluation. We encourage a diversity of perspectives and experiences within each volume, as well as creative bridges between evaluation and other sectors of our collective lives.

The editors do not consider or publish unsolicited single manuscripts. Each issue of the journal is devoted to a single topic, with contributions solicited, organized, reviewed, and edited by a guest editor. Issues may take any of several forms, such as a series of related chapters, a debate, or a long article followed by brief critical commentaries. In all cases, the proposals must follow a specific format, which can be obtained from the editor-in-chief. These proposals are sent to members of the editorial board and to relevant substantive experts for peer review. The process may result in acceptance, a recommendation to revise and resubmit, or rejection. However, the editors are committed to working constructively with potential guest editors to help them develop acceptable proposals.

Jennifer C. Greene, Editor-in-Chief
Department of Policy Analysis and Management
Cornell University
Ithaca, NY 14853–4401
e-mail: jcg8@cornell.edu

Gary T. Henry, Editor-in-Chief
School of Policy Studies
Georgia State University
P.O. Box 4039
Atlanta, GA 30302–4039
e-mail: gthenry@gsu.edu

CONTENTS

CONTENTS

EDITOR'S NOTES

Evaluation practice, like any social practice, is socioculturally and historically determined. Understandings of the practice differ from country to country, depending upon institutional arrangements, intellectual traditions, and political practices. For example, House (1993) has explored the role of evaluation practices in legitimating government actions in different kinds of capitalist societies. As another example, when Rist (1989–1990, 1990) compared government-related evaluation activities in the United States, Britain, Canada, Germany, Norway, Denmark, the Netherlands, and Switzerland, he pointed out several differences; these included the degree of centralization of evaluation practices, the degree of evaluator independence, the degree of access to evaluation reports, the degree of affiliation with auditing organizations, and the type of unit (executive or legislative) to which evaluators report.

The chapters in this volume provide many insights into Scandinavians' understanding of their own evaluation practices. Of course, there is no single "Scandinavian" perspective on evaluation any more than there is a single "American" perspective on the topic. Yet, it is undeniable that evaluation theory and practice in Norway, Sweden, and Denmark unfold against a set of sociocultural circumstances and intellectual influences that differ in many important respects from those in America.

For example, in Scandinavian countries, there is no distinct, separate social science specialty in evaluation. Some government agencies have evaluation units (for example, the Swedish National Agency for Education), but for the most part, evaluators ply their trade from within their specialty. That is, as social researchers, they both acquire and apply their skills by describing, explaining, and critiquing the issues, problems, and policies within their field or discipline—be it education, social security, disability, industrial development, sociology, economics, or another area. Furthermore, at least some of these disciplines have been far less influenced than their U.S. counterparts by the legacy of logical empiricism, whereas they have been far more influenced by Continental philosophy.

Perhaps more important, Scandinavian evaluation practice unfolds against a sociopolitical backdrop and in the context of a polity that is considerably different from the United States. This difference is often summed up by the sweeping characterization of Scandinavian countries as exemplars of the social democratic welfare state. But that label tells us very little.

Two features of this form of government (and this type of political theory and social policy) seem to play particularly important roles in the issues raised in this volume. First, the welfare state in Scandinavia (and Europe, more generally) has always been defined in political and ideological terms and has been viewed as a matter of choice based on principles of equality and solidarity.

Developing social policy in such a framework has largely been seen as an exercise of statecraft. In contrast, in the United States, the commitment to social welfare has largely been viewed in technocratic terms, with social policy being something like an exercise in social technology. In the Scandinavian context, fashioning a welfare system has generally meant developing and sustaining policies and practices that would provide basic services and support to all its citizens. Scandinavians generally view poverty, unemployment, and other "social problems" as structural; they regard "social engineering" as a strategy for "repairing" whatever is wrong with society. In the United States, people typically see issues such as unemployment and poverty as originating with an individual; "social engineering" has generally meant helping individuals and groups overcome those problems so that they can function more effectively within a liberal market-based society (Mishra, 1984).

Second, in the past two decades or so, the welfare states of Norway, Sweden, and Denmark have been in crisis. The precise nature of that crisis varies from country to country, but it generally has to do with reforms that challenge the state's strong central role in helping society achieve equality and solidarity. *Decentralization, modernization,* and *deregulation* are reform watchwords. Authority and responsibility for social welfare (and reform) have been shifted to local levels of the political structure. Extensive laws and regulations are being simplified in response to criticisms of an inflexible, highly bureaucratic, centralized state. What is also being strongly challenged is the assumption that professionals in all fields (education, social services administration, psychology, and so forth) can help "repair" society through expert knowledge.

Of course, decentralization and deregulation are familiar notions in the contemporary U.S. debate about governance (although this volume is not devoted to exploring how these notions vary across political cultures). Nevertheless, it is important to recognize that this volume's chapter authors write in the context of the welfare state's legacy and current reform efforts. Some deal with these issues explicitly, others implicitly, but such matters are undeniably present in their discussions of evaluation practice.

One way in which this background manifests itself in all the chapters (except for the last one, perhaps) is in terms of a challenge to evaluators' authority as experts and a challenge to evaluation as a distinctively different kind of professional conduct. Most of the authors suggest that evaluation ought to be more of a sophisticated way of questioning what society is up to than a particular methodology or set of technical skills. Furthermore, the authors emphasize using evaluation activities for understanding and reflecting. They suggest that evaluation (and social research, more broadly) may have its greatest significance not simply in the questions it raises (and the answers it provides) but in the attitudes, interests, and debates it cultivates by virtue of the questions it raises (Telhaug, 1995).

In the opening chapter, Peder Haug, who directs a large-scale, long-term project examining Norway's special education reforms and current policies, writes about how the current sociopolitical climate and current reform strategies in education affect evaluation practice. He believes that it is inadequate to link evaluation (or, more generally, social science research) to social policy-making through technocratic approaches. He defends an approach developed in Sweden called "theory-oriented evaluation"; this requires the evaluator to serve as a kind of public intellectual offering knowledge of social programming that is both critical and geared toward the future.

In Chapter Two, the focus shifts from Norway to Sweden. Ove Karlsson, a social researcher, argues for a theory of evaluation that will fit with the growing pluralism of the Swedish welfare state's social policy. In Karlsson's view, more and more stakeholders are demanding to be heard in the formation of social policy. Yet he finds that traditional stakeholder evaluation approaches accommodate those interests inadequately. He argues that evaluation conceptualized and practiced as a process of critical dialogue would better fit the political and social realities of Swedish policymaking.

In Chapter Three, Linda Andersen, a member of the Adult Education Research Group at Roskilde University, broadly critiques the modernization of the Danish welfare state. This modernization consists of a series of reforms begun in the 1980s to improve the public sector's productivity and efficiency. She is particularly interested in what these reforms conceal as well as what they reveal. In Chapter Three, she argues that evaluators must understand how an evaluation strategy and methodology are situated in the different discourses of modernity.

In Chapter Four, Finn Hansson, a social researcher, uses C. P. Snow's concept of two cultures as a framework. From there, Hansson relates the historical development of Danish evaluation research to struggles over the definition and institutional location of Danish sociology. He also reviews current evaluation research in terms of three models for the production and use of knowledge in society.

The first four chapters examine issues of evaluation theory and methodology in the context of education and human service programs and the reform policies associated with such programs in the welfare state. In Chapter Five, Hans Torvatn, a researcher in the Institute of Social Research in Industry, examines the history and current practice of evaluation in industrial development in Norway. Torvatn's chapter provides some important insights into the connections between evaluation practice and the Norwegian tradition of action research.

Thomas A. Schwandt
Editor

References

House, E. R. *Professional Evaluation: Social and Political Consequences.* Thousand Oaks, Calif.: Sage, 1993.
Mishra, R. *The Welfare State in Crisis: Social Thought and Social Change.* New York: St. Martin's Press, 1984.

Rist, R. C. "On the Application of Program Evaluation Designs: Sorting Out Their Use and Abuse." *Knowledge in Society,* 1989–1990, 2 (4), 74–96.

Rist, R. C. (ed.). *Program Evaluation and the Management of Government.* New Brunswick, N.J.: Transaction Books, 1990.

Telhaug, A. O. "A Norwegian Perspective on Swedish Policy for School Research." In A. Tuijnman and E. Wallin (eds.), *School Research at the Crossroads: Swedish and Nordic Perspectives.* Stockholm: Stockholm Institute of Education Press, 1995.

THOMAS A. SCHWANDT *is associate professor of education at Indiana University and coordinator of the Educational Inquiry Methodology Program.*

The current philosophy and politics of social reform strategies in Norway pose unique challenges and opportunities for evaluation theory.

Linking Evaluation and Reform Strategies

Peder Haug

My concern is the relationship between political processes and evaluation. I will examine how some important contemporary governmental reforms are developed, decided, and implemented in Norway and how evaluation may be affected by this process. The core of my argument is that the development of reforms in the 1990s differs from strategies used in earlier periods. A new, united, and clearly outspoken reform strategy is being implemented. This in turn has posed particularly significant challenges for evaluation.

Intention, Situation, and Definition

My intention is to develop an understanding of evaluation by discussing and analyzing the external and internal demands made on evaluation in recent Norwegian reform experiences. This is a pragmatic approach to understanding evaluation, differing, for instance, from discussions of the logic of evaluation (Scriven, 1995).

The definition and practice of evaluation depend on the context in which it functions, as well as on the societal game in which it is played (Smith, 1995). In practice, evaluation is influenced by two types of factors. Cultural and political requests influence evaluation externally. The researcher does not control these external demands, which establish how much space is available for realizing goals and what options exist. These expectations can be explicit but can just as well be woven into subtler social and cultural structures, making them vague, general, and difficult to grasp, as has often been the case. More often than not, these external expectations conflict. Different groups of stakeholders, for instance, often have completely different needs and requirements. The result is that there are frequently significant and competing demands for evaluation that are difficult to satisfy.

The internal determinants concern the professional ideals of the evaluation community. These ideals influence who evaluates (institution and profession), what theme can be taken up in evaluation (territory), what kind of substantial understanding constitutes the basis for the evaluation (theory), what strategies and methods are used (methodology), and what results are expected (use).

Evaluation has countless meanings and forms. There is no widespread consensus on how it should be defined or used. This "confusion" is perhaps even greater in Scandinavia than in the United States, for example, because Scandinavians have no coordinated discussion and tradition of evaluating reforms. We have no specialized evaluation journals in Scandinavia, and evaluation is not an independent field. It is almost always subordinated to the substantive field or discipline in which one is educated or employed. The debate on evaluation is therefore primarily a matter for different areas of research, not for a separately constituted field of evaluation.

Thus far in Scandinavia, there has been little interest in unifying and consolidating the concept of evaluation or in developing a shared and broader theory of evaluation across the disciplines. Nor is there any great interest in gathering areas of evaluation into a single community or organization. The desire among those who work with evaluation seems to be to let the many flowers bloom more or less freely. This makes it more difficult to orient oneself and to achieve a broad perspective on the issues. This has had a great impact on evaluation. In particular, it has had several significant consequences for the development of the field in Scandinavia.

When Scandinavian specialists try to clarify the traditions of evaluation, it becomes clear that they are primarily familiar with those that have developed within their own fields. Pedagogues have their tradition, sociologists theirs, psychologists theirs, economists theirs, and so on.

When evaluation practice is centered in a discipline, substantive issues tend to receive greater attention than methodological ones. Of course, the disciplines in Scandinavia have also been the site of methodological quarrels and are by no means free from methodological "tyranny." The way in which methodological debate has dominated the U.S. field of evaluation is not characteristic of Scandinavian evaluation practice, though.

At the same time, the representatives of different disciplines build models independently and simultaneously. Each defines the term *evaluation* according to his or her own professional needs and ideas, while having no special knowledge of how others are approaching the matter. This contributes to the proliferation of different forms, strategies, and understandings of evaluation. In a superficial analysis, these can seem more similar than they are.

Another important fact is that the Scandinavian research community is not very large. Most often, the same institutions and researchers are continually engaged both in research and evaluation. In the long run, they become associated with each other, blurring the boundary between research and evaluation, making them more alike.

My contribution here is a modest attempt to create a more common point of departure, but I am not at all convinced that what we need is a common understanding or a single theory or logic of evaluation.

Scriven (1991) defined evaluation as either the process of determining something's merit, worth, or value, or the result of that process. This definition is largely accepted and widely used. I do not disagree with Scriven's requirement of determining merit, worth, or value, but I question how to transfer these formulations into the Norwegian practice of evaluation as I know it. In this chapter, I will explore this issue using examples from Norwegian evaluations and will focus on three central disputes in evaluation:

1. Should the evaluator only make value judgments and not explain?
2. Is it the evaluator's responsibility to make a summative judgment of value after synthesizing evidence?
3. Must an evaluator have at least an implicit theory of political context in order to do good evaluation?

Use of Evaluation

I will approach the Norwegian situation by briefly discussing different conceptions of evaluation's use and function. The notion of utilization is central to an understanding of how evaluation is legitimated. The term *utilization* in evaluation research is very complex (Alkin, 1990; Cousins and Leithwood, 1986; Smith, 1988), but I will discuss three ways of understanding it: instrumental, interactive, and legitimizing utilization.

Instrumental Utilization. According to Brunsson and Olsen (1990), a strong political and administrative Scandinavian tradition has shaped the development and implementation of reforms, in which evaluation plays an integral part. This dominating perspective of reforms is characterized by terms such as *centralist, rational, instrumental, technical,* and *top-down.*

In a narrow sense, instrumental utilization in this tradition means that evaluation should prescribe possible corrective steps to ensure that a reform process takes a required direction and achieves the reform's stated goals. A wider and more general meaning is that the evaluation results should enable the contractor to introduce some form of observable change in the reform.

The epistemological notions behind these expectations can be traced back to logical empiricism. The presupposition is that the evaluation reveals the "objective" truth about the reform; on that ground, it is rationally possible to direct the reform processes. There have been many debates on this issue within evaluation, both philosophically (for example, Guba, 1990) and with respect to the specific question of use (for example, Alkin, 1990; Patton, 1988a, 1988b; Weiss, 1988a, 1988b).

Contrary to the assumptions underlying the notion of instrumental utility, the available evidence indicates that reform development and use of evaluation are extremely complex issues that depend on a wide range of factors (Cousins and Leithwood, 1986; March and Olsen, 1989; Smith, 1988). The more comprehensive, complicated, political, and controversial the case, the more difficult it becomes to validate an evaluation from a technical, rational, and instrumental point of view (for example, Weiler, 1989).

Interactive Utilization. In order to meet the demands represented by the substantial, ethical, moral, cultural, and political ambiguities, ambivalences, disagreements, and dilemmas associated with reforms and evaluation, the reform literature presents several alternatives to instrumental use through such concepts as enlightenment (Weiss, 1970), understanding (Stake, 1986), or empowerment (Fetterman, 1994). Others, such as Schwandt (1997) and Karlsson (Chapter Two of this volume), introduce different definitions of *dialogue* as a way to use evaluation.

In principle, what all these very different approaches have in common is a conviction that evaluation knowledge cannot and should not dictate decisions. On the contrary, it is through different kinds of interactions, negotiations, reflections, struggles, and arguments that people develop policy, select and implement reforms, and "use" evaluation. Hence, interaction utilization is the concept I choose for this particular understanding of evaluation's use and function.

In practice, this interaction often is not developed as far as it might or should be, despite the fact that open interaction on matters such as governmental reforms should be compulsory in a democracy. The role of evaluation in this struggle can vary from one evaluation strategy to the next, but the goal is to feed substantial knowledge into the public arena to stimulate and inform discussants and stakeholders.

Evaluation research can produce arguments and knowledge and thus support different types of interaction. Such research cannot solve problems or give the "right" answers. It can only present perspectives on the problems to ensure an intelligent, critical, and democratic interaction with the aims of developing as far as possible a common understanding and reaching acceptable solutions. In this sense, evaluation can help us identify new problems or modify our understanding of old ones. It can do so by diagnosing social injustice, asking surprising and difficult questions, contributing to wider perspectives on matters, and developing, widening, or narrowing concepts.

Legitimizing Utilization. There are two types of legitimization use of evaluation: strategic use and symbolic use. *Strategic use* occurs when evaluation results are presented to support opinions and decisions that have already been made on other grounds. *Symbolic use* means that the central issue is not the concrete evaluation result but rather the fact that an evaluation has been performed. That at least gives the impression that the process leading to the decisions has been thorough and rational. This gives the institutions and the people involved in the decisions legitimacy and prestige, independent of how the evaluation results are adopted. Theoretically, all evaluations can work this way. Legitimization is far more common than instrumental use (Sabatier, 1986).

Three Reform Periods

My point of departure is the experience of evaluating Norwegian educational reforms. The main reform strategies I will describe can be found in Norway's whole state sector and are not unique to education. The concept of reform is complex. I lean heavily here on Weiler's definition (1985) of *educational reform* as "the initiation, modification, implementation, and/or nonimplementation of policies designed to change the 'social product' of the educational process along the lines of ideological and political priorities of certain groups in society" (p. 169). Not surprisingly, reforms can also have symbolic functions, in which case it is more important to make decisions than to implement them (Brunsson, 1989). These are not the kind of reforms I am concerned with here. I focus on real attempts to make profound changes, not on legitimization or symbolic gesture in which the point is only to draw attention to a matter, a person, a political party, or an institution and not to effect change and development.

Norwegian reform policy has gone through three distinct periods since the 1950s, reflecting differences in the processes behind the reforms, in the ways the reforms are implemented, and in the way evaluation has been used. These three periods coincide with three phases in the development of the Scandinavian welfare state. The concept of a welfare state is quite diffuse. Here I take it to mean the state's role in securing individual rights and equality in, among other things, health care, social services, and education. The first period is the golden age, the second is the great disappointment, and the third is an attempt at restoration.

Centralized reforms (1950–1975). In the first period, there was a close collaboration between the departmental specialists and the educational authorities—the teachers' union and the Education Committee in Parliament. These three groups were also called the "iron triangle" or "triangle of tension" (Ball, 1994). The strategies were a combination of top-down technical instrumentalism and pragmatism. Very often, large public committees considered the reform problems. The main strategy was to reach a detailed consensus on aims and means in the committees. These goals could be supplied or supported by small-scale experiments. What the committees recommended was almost always adopted in Parliament.

The formal role of evaluation at that time was to assist instrumentally in reaching the goals. Evaluation was heavily instrumental, quantitative, and product oriented. Frequently, evaluation only had legitimizing functions and did not influence the reforms at all. On some occasions, evaluation was not done, even if it was required.

For a while, this reform strategy seemed to function very well, but that did not last long. In the late 1960s, it became clear that the welfare state no longer gave what it had promised. Centralized strategies used to reach welfare state goals were called into question. Education was expanded and huge amounts of money were put into education, but the results did not correspond to expectations. Instead, lots of problems became apparent, including increasing behavior problems, low achievement, and so forth, a situation also found in many other countries (Coombs, 1968) and in other fields. The reform strategy, the evaluation approach, and the state's responsibility were all criticized. The ultimate question was whether the state could ensure public well-being.

Inner reforms (1970–1990). In opposition to this centralized and, in certain ways, technical and instrumental reform strategy, a populist and idealistic notion of decentralization and public participation gradually developed. The responsibility for choosing and implementing reform policy was given at least partly to counties and municipalities. The central government and the Parliament were to draw the big lines as before, but "the people" in the communities were to realize the policy according to local standards, needs, and traditions.

Evaluation played no central role in this strategy. Some evaluations were done, but most were informal. Often, they were not reported in writing or they were inaccessible to larger audiences. Evaluation was more intuitive, internal, and qualitative, as well as instrumental and process oriented. The evaluator was frequently the same person who was responsible for implementing the program or reform. For policy development, the function of evaluation was still mainly to legitimate.

It may be asked to what extent this decentralization actually took place. What did take place has been labeled "decentralized centralism" (Karlsen, 1993), meaning that the local communities did not obtain power and opportunities to influence the reforms, as promised. This reform strategy also had its weaknesses; the results of these "inner reforms" were not what people expected. The notion of the welfare state was still challenged by a lack of development in the desired direction. The most serious problem was an alleged decrease in educational quality. Once again, reform strategy, evaluation approach, and state responsibility were highly criticized and questioned.

Fast, complex, rational, political ad hoc idealism (1990–). During the 1980s, a new reform model had to be developed. In addition to what has already been mentioned, the motivation for this change was to subdue and exclude corporate pressure and to bring out political and idealistic interests, in conformity with results from the Norwegian study entitled *Distribution of Power* (Norwegian Official Information, 1982, p. 3).

A new, very competent, and highly influential minister of education, Gudmund Hernes, was appointed in 1990. As a professor of sociology, this minister also had led the study of the distribution of power. He, more than anyone else, publicly formulated and presented the governmental strategy of reform, the metalevel program theory that has been adopted during the 1990s. From some of his speeches and from his reforms, I have extracted six elements characterizing this reform strategy. Together, they are a combination of what I label a "fast, complex, rational, political ad hoc idealistic reform process."

1. *Prepare the reforms on an idealistic basis.* An idealistic model of reform is concerned with the intellectual challenges involved in the process of change. In this perspective, developing a reform primarily means cognitively coordinating dissimilar interests and conceptions in an intellectually honest way. A diagnosis is formulated, and different courses of action are defined and then prioritized on the basis of rational intellectual evaluations. The challenge is to solve the problem rationally both through imaginative vision and facts. Idealism's strength lies on the intellectual level. It is characterized by comprehensive collection and analysis of data. It is also particularly advantageous in that this model is independent of interest groups. In some cases, it is just as independent as research can be.

2. *Prepare the reforms on a political basis.* In accordance with this principle, the reforms are mostly prepared and worked out in political parties, departments, governmental, and parliamentary committees. Experts outside the political arenas are much less engaged in preparing the reforms. For a minority government, this is an important part of reaching political consensus, as we have had in Norway for many years now. The actual reform in question must be developed through processes in which purely formal political interests influence the reform. Therefore, a large degree of consensus appears that is nonetheless associated with ideas and not with practical execution. The goal in this form of political consensus activity is to arrive at a common resolution in the political arena.

3. *When a reform is adopted, changes are implemented first, and then people must be convinced that the reform is in their best interest.* In some instances, the implementation of reforms starts long before they are decided on by Parliament. Reforming the other way around—first using the discursive strategy to convince people, then going through with the changes, as was used in earlier times—is believed to be much more difficult and produces much more resistance.

4. *Implement the reforms as quickly as possible.* In a speech to an audience of researchers, the minister once said (partly as a provocation) that reforms should be implemented so quickly that when the researchers present their evaluation showing the effects or lack of effects, the results will be outdated. The reform will already have been altered, and the research will no longer be accurate or deal with the most crucial issues. His message was that speed in itself is important to avoid resistance and to reach the reform goals.

5. *Reforms should be complex.* Simple changes tend to be overrun by the established and unchanged part of the systems under reform. The reforms must make deep and substantial changes to old, established, and tradition-bound institutions. According to the new institutionalism, organizations such as schools have developed standard means of meeting new challenges (Crawson, Boyd, and Mawhinney, 1996). More often than not, organizations do not

do this by implementing the intended changes. Rather than altering working methods, they effect change by undertaking new tasks—for instance, adopting new ways of talking (Brunsson, 1989). When people make complex and comprehensive changes, it is much more difficult to survey it all. Therefore, it is also much more difficult for others to resist change.

6. *This strategy leads to frequent debates, developments, and modifications during implementation, which then become an extension of the policymaking process.* As implementation proceeds, people might make changes to the reforms. This situation is inevitable because the basic problem is how to implement a purely political and idealistic reform when it has not been tried out before, when the experts have not discussed it, when the personnel who are going to do the actual work do not necessarily show support, and when the different stakeholder groups have not had the opportunity to present their understandings and concerns about the reform. Therefore, these reforms are continuously evaluated to ensure that they develop in the direction desired. Evaluations are fed back to the central administration, as well as to the public to be engaged in interactions, to decide what responses are appropriate and on what arenas and levels. Because this is a continuous process, evaluation is a central part of the interactions around the policymaking process and assumes a direct role in both the formulation and implementation of governmental decisions. A pragmatic strategy, which in earlier days was reflected in committee work and in small-scale experiments before reforms were chosen and implemented, must now be enacted as part of the implementation process to a greater extent.

Several educational reforms have been and will be carried out in this way in Norway in the 1990s, including the reform in compulsory school starting in 1997, the reform in upper secondary school started in 1994, and the reform in higher education started in 1992. All these reforms are highly complex and include institutional reorganization, new ways of management, new curricula, and changed ideals and intentions in teaching and learning. The changes are profound, and the new requirements for the institutions and staff are very comprehensive and challenging. The reorganization has been carried out thoroughly and quickly. The changes are so large that it is almost impossible to describe, understand, or assess the reforms. For that matter, it is difficult to obtain a detailed understanding of what they involve from simple methods or direct empirical information.

Another main criticism has been that these reforms are too unformulated to be implemented. The political opposition and the teachers' unions have argued that the reforms should have been postponed until plans and preparations were improved, but this has not been supported. The minister once responded to the criticism by saying that we have to "build the plane while flying," which meant that he did not want to make or believe in making detailed plans beforehand.

It could be interesting to follow up on several aspects of this reform strategy. One such aspect is the heavy marketing of the reforms. To obtain political consensus, politicians have to market reform proposals. It is always easy to promise too much and to make the reforms seem much more important and promising than they actually are. Governmental reforms are often much less successful than people expect them to be (Haug, 1996).

Challenges for Evaluation

How should the field of evaluation react to the situation described above? The challenge for evaluation is to play its part in the societal game and, at the same time, to live up to external expectations and internal professional ideals. The complexity and difficulty of this task as seen from the political arena can be explained by two dilemmas presented by the minister of education. First, the minister wanted two sorts of evaluations. Gathering "steering data" meant continuously collecting statistical data that gave detailed information about the developments. The ministerial bureaucracy and the National Statistical Bureau were responsible for accomplishing this task. The second type of evaluation, "accompanying research," was more thorough. It involved asking two questions.

1. *Is the reform working?* The minister required information about the reform development, not only according to previously established criteria but also in other areas that could be important for both implementation and outcomes.

2. *Why is the reform developing as it is?* In this request for evaluation, the minister seemed to go beyond the definition of evaluation as a determination of worth and merit. He wanted information about why things were going as they were. The reason was obvious. The minister was supposed to participate in a public debate about the reform and was expected to modify reform directives. It was insufficient for him simply to know what was going on and whether things were advancing according to plans and intentions.

He required explanations, but not just any explanation. He wanted relevant and critical perspectives from the research—perspectives that would tell him something he did not know or expect. He wanted "more powerful thoughts in a more vigorous language," and he sought, among other things, a big "aha experience" that could bring forward new understanding and explain problems in challenging ways. In terms of managing the reform process, he felt that it was difficult and possibly counterproductive to interact and act without understanding. Evaluation could help avoid this.

Despite this call for evaluations that would help explain reforms, the minister was critical of the evaluations that sought to develop this understanding. He commented that evaluators frequently used too much time to produce presentable results. In several cases, evaluations came in after decisions had been made. In the political arena, the minister often had to act quickly. Instead of using evaluations, he had to work with the information at hand. Sometimes, he could only obtain information by calling someone he trusted or someone with knowledge of the field. It was a method he disliked, but in some cases he saw no other alternative.

He felt that some of the evaluations being done were of such low quality that he, as a professor of sociology, could not accept them. The researchers, he said, showed an astounding lack of substantial knowledge about the institutions and problems they were evaluating. They might have been highly skilled in research methods, but that was not sufficient.

From the evaluator's point of view, it is difficult to know whether this claim of low speed and quality reflects results that the minister did not like, or whether the studies really were poor. The community of evaluators has criticized both the conditions in which they must perform evaluations and the minister's own assessment of the evaluation studies. They have claimed that when their evaluation results contradict political interests, the research is sometimes critiqued as having low quality. This pronouncement of the evaluation's inadequacy then serves to legitimize political decisions.

The different perspectives presented here are general issues in evaluation, and several researchers have reported this situation in the past. The scientist and the politician inhabit two different worlds and have different ideals, needs, and attitudes regarding evaluation and its use. In any case, the scene is set: evaluation must be done professionally, very quickly, with high quality, and in a way that would prevent political misuse. Evaluation should take into account the diversity of interests and values related to the general public welfare and contribute to political and public interaction on these issues. Is all this possible?

Without a doubt, the external requirements for evaluation in the present reform strategy are complicated. It seems difficult, perhaps even impossible, to meet demands such as this; the minister of education might want the unattainable. One might suspect that the role of evaluation is actually formulated for strategic and symbolic reasons. On the one hand, it can then be stated that if evaluation is done, it must be of very high quality. On the other hand, if evaluation is not done, it is because it is almost impossible for research to answer any of the difficult questions raised during a reform process. In both cases, the arguments would legitimize the action and decisions chosen.

Theory-Oriented Evaluation

In my opinion, these requirements for evaluation could be met in a scientifically honest way, but the approach I am presenting is in no way unproblematic. The strategy is demanding and presupposes a high degree of competence and professionalism. The most important prerequisite is that evaluation not be a separate professional field, as Scriven (1995) and others have argued. "General" evaluators would not fit in the present Norwegian context. What we need is not so much technical and methodological expertise but substantive knowledge of the problem under study, as is generally the case in social research. Therefore, evaluation must be subordinated to the discipline within which the evaluation is done, as is the Norwegian tradition. To meet the formulated demands, the evaluation must be done by a highly skilled researcher. This person must master the field in which the evaluation is done (education, sociology, and so forth), have profound knowledge of the institutions in which the reform takes place (schools, universities, and so on), have an in-depth knowledge of reforms in this sector, and master the problems and tasks of evaluation.

The theory-oriented approach to evaluation is one way of achieving this goal (Haug, 1992). This understanding or strategy of evaluation emphasizes theoretical orientations and theoretical explanations far more than has traditionally been the case (House, 1994). The strategy advocates theory in evaluation, a field that still can be seen as largely oriented away from theory and toward methodology.

The theory-oriented approach is not equivalent to the theory-driven or theory-based evaluation of, for instance, Chen (1990) and Freeman and Rossi (1993). In theory-driven evaluation, the main purpose is to test hypotheses derived from social science in order to build general theories about social problems. Likewise, a theory-oriented approach must be distinguished from the idea of formulating program theory on the basis of the stakeholders' opinions of how a reform will work (Alkin, 1991).

The school of thought I present and represent is based on a critical, hermeneutic understanding of science. Theory-oriented evaluation comes from the Swedish theory tradition in evaluation (Dahllöf, 1967; Franke-Wikberg and Lundgren, 1979; Lundgren, 1978). This is a conceptualization of evaluation corresponding to the rationality closely related to the present governmental reform strategies. It has its origin in the close cooperation between politicians and evaluators in the big Swedish education reforms, which in some respects were similar to what is now happening in Norway. The main emphasis of this approach is to analyze a reform in order to determine what influences it, how it works, and how it functions in society. The evaluation strategy is characterized by the six elements I will now describe (see also Haug, 1997).

Explicit Statement of Theory Basis. The aim of evaluation is to give a broader understanding of how reforms are shaped and what functions they serve in relation to society and the individual. Therefore, evaluation must be based on extensive knowledge about or theories of the phenomenon under study. The more complex the reform and its context, the larger the need to express theoretical perspectives as the basis for valuing and knowing, which are not "objective" processes. Theoretical perspectives are a way to explain and understand how the processes and results of reforms are connected to a wide range of organizational, social, political, and cultural conditions.

Theory-based evaluation also means providing information about the values underlying the evaluations. Values affect at least two arenas of evaluation—formulation and realization. In both arenas, an evaluation must identify and address several sets of values, including the social, cultural, and political values behind a reform; the corresponding values in a reform; the different stakeholder values; and the researcher's values as a professional in the field. The researcher's values are important, because they will affect the questions asked, the ways of posing them, and the ways of interpreting the answers. By making these values as explicit as possible, the evaluator provides the different stakeholders and the contractor with a point of departure for their own understanding and discussion of results. Values are embedded in these theoretical concepts and explanations of reform functions more than in explicit value statements.

Analysis of Reform and Results. The main aim of evaluation is to describe the processes and results of the reform analytically and then to use theory to explain the results as they appear. The view of research and what it can contribute changes from pure, concrete, short-term thinking about utility to an emphasis on expertise and expanding knowledge. The aim is not to assert what should be done to secure the development of reforms. Knowledge alone will not change the development of the reform. The contribution is rather to identify and clarify problems addressed by the reform, the relationships between them, and the consequences they have. This analysis can always be challenged, which will often happen in a public interaction.

Consideration of Context. One of the key questions is to what extent forces outside the reform influence the reform itself and the evaluation. There is a growing understanding that sources outside the field at hand influence what happens within the field. Therefore, a contextual perspective is important. Sabatier (1987), for instance, distinguishes between stable context factors and dynamic context factors. The stable context factors include the more fundamental cultural and judicial values in society, the historical conditions, and so on. The dynamic context factors change more quickly but still have a lot of influence. Examples include technological innovation, socioeconomic conditions, views of knowledge, and so on.

The social democratic Scandinavian culture and tradition will permit and expect very different approaches and more explicit statements of values than the far more pluralistic and "neutral" U.S. culture (Haug, 1997). This shows how much the internal scientific conditions and priorities depend on the external social expectations. This dependence also puts into perspective the matter of whose interests an evaluation will represent. An evaluation of a reform according to a contextual model will provide a partial explanation of why a certain reform develops as it does.

Study of Institution's History. Most often, governmental reforms change or expand already established agreements and institutions. In this situation, institutional traditions play a central role, both in affecting what is happening and in resisting or accepting change (March and Olsen, 1989). The past provides the framework for a substantial part of our everyday experiences. Therefore, a historically inclined study is a natural part of the evaluation of a present and concrete reform. History is one of the most important context factors we have (see, for example, Durkheim, 1977; Goodson, 1988).

Critical Analysis of Interests Served. In a theory-oriented strategy, the evaluator must question the phenomena at hand and try to find an alternative understanding and explanation. The aim must be to clarify whose interests are being served by a certain reform and by certain evaluation results. One must not take the marketing of reform at face value but must discuss in detail whether the promises are realistic (Lindensjö and Lundgren, 1986). In a Norwegian context, it would also be natural for the evaluator to side with the weaker party and to be especially aware of its problems and needs.

There is often a lack of consensus around the aims and actions of reforms. They are frequently the result of struggles and compromises, making them contradictory and vague. The evaluator needs to enter these conflicts and clarify how the different interests have developed. The evaluator should also map the views and experiences of the different stakeholders.

Examination of Reform Process. Because of the relationship between stated goals and realization that I have discussed, there is a need to map and analyze what happens *during* a reform process, not simply what happens as a *result* of that process. The results can only be explained through a thorough understanding of what has taken place (Dahllöf, 1967).

Norwegian educational reforms are often not evaluated according to student achievement, as is the case in many other countries. For reasons of equality, the policy for a very long time has been that of securing opportunity and input more than of measuring result. In the context of the welfare state, it has been more important to establish whether values such as the following are present: equal participation, allocation of resources according to need, equality between genders, a balance of languages in the curriculum, and so forth. This policy is often best studied as several processes rather than as end products.

Conclusion

This chapter does not give a complete picture of Norwegian evaluation, but I have presented some aspects of the evaluation of educational reforms. Some of the points I have made have relevance for the evaluation debates in the United States. In this concluding part of the chapter, I will comment briefly on several issues.

To function within a defined political context, evaluation must balance the external political and cultural demands and the evaluation community's internal definitions and standards. To function in the Norwegian situation, evaluation therefore must include an aspect of explanation. This idea contradicts what others (Scriven, 1995, for instance) argue—that an evaluation should only value, not explain.

At least to a certain degree, evaluation in Norway is structured and organized to meet a substantive field's demands for knowledge. Evaluators are recruited for their substantive merits and are expected to work in fields in which they are experts. This makes evaluators capable of investigating reforms in very different ways than would be true if they did not know the field. This is also critical to the theory orientation. As we have seen, even with this framework, evaluation has been criticized for evaluators' lack of substantial knowledge about the institutions they study.

For a long time, the U.S. debate has wrestled with the question of value statements. The debate involves two opposing views: (1) the evaluator should make a summative judgment of merit or worth based on evidence (House,

1995; Scriven, 1995) or (2) the evaluator should not make a summative judgment of merit or worth based on evidence but should instead describe various judgments. Then it is up to the various stakeholders to decide how they will judge value (Shadish, Cook, and Leviton, 1991).

There are no principles in theory-oriented evaluation that prevent making summative judgments of merit or worth. On the contrary, one main argument behind this strategy is to gain a better holistic view of and grip on the reform, its background, its context, and its results. In principle, therefore, the theory orientation supports the first view, not the second. The main question, however, is not whether the evaluator should render a judgment but whether a single summative judgment—that is, a synthesis—is possible.

The examples of synthesis supplied by Scriven (1995) and House (1995) deal with very simple tasks that are not comparable to the big, complex reforms I discuss here. The strength of theory-oriented evaluation as described here is to study reforms simultaneously on several levels and in several arenas with different research strategies and theoretical approaches, varying from individual-oriented microstudies to comprehensive institutional and societal macrostudies. Often, it is neither meaningful to synthesize substudies of this kind nor possible to synthesize across societal levels and arenas in an honest way. When a goal of evaluation is to contribute to interaction utilization, it is not helpful or informative to give a single statement about the developments and values of complex reforms. To be taken seriously, the field of evaluation must not hide that fact, I believe. Therefore, a single thumbs-up or thumbs-down made according to criteria fixed beforehand is not that interesting or illuminating in these cases. Such an approach is almost always a form of reductionism that negatively affects the interaction processes by making the reform developments, results, and values appear more settled when, in fact, they are diffuse and unclear.

Scriven (1993) and others have argued that a theory of evaluation should not and need not include a theory of political context. The Norwegian situation I have described clearly shows that the political context is an integral part of the reform being evaluated and that the evaluation also has clear political functions as the reform is implemented. We have seen that reform results are often closely linked to program decisions. This means that an evaluation of a governmental reform should also include an analysis of the political processes and interests behind the reform being studied. On the one hand, this can produce knowledge that can increase the understanding of the reform developments. On the other hand, it also opens values behind the reform to further investigation and therefore fosters inquiry into whose interests the reform will serve.

References

Alkin, M. C. *Debates on Evaluation*. Thousand Oaks, Calif.: Sage, 1990.
Alkin, M. C. "Education Theory Development." In M. W. McLaughlin and D. C. Phillips (eds.), *Evaluation and Education: At Quarter Century*. Chicago: University of Chicago Press, 1991.
Ball, S. *Educational Reform*. Bristol, Pa.: Open University Books, 1994.

Brunsson, N. *The Organization of Hypocrisy.* New York: Wiley, 1989.

Brunsson, N., and Olsen, J. P. *Makten at reformera* [The power to make reforms]. Stockholm: Carlsson, 1990.

Chen, H.-T. *Theory-Driven Evaluations: A Comprehensive Perspective.* Thousand Oaks, Calif.: Sage, 1990.

Coombs, P. H. *The World Educational Crisis: A Systems Analysis.* New York: Oxford University Press, 1968.

Cousins, J. B., and Leithwood, K. A. "Current Research on Evaluation Utilization." *Review of Educational Research,* 1986, *56* (3), 331–364.

Crawson, R. L., Boyd, W. L., and Mawhinney, H. B. *The Politics of Education and the New Institutionalism.* Bristol, Pa.: Falmer Press, 1996.

Dahllöf, U. *Skoldifferentiering och undervisningsförlop* [Differentiation in school and teaching]. Stockholm: Almquist & Wiksell, 1967.

Durkheim, E. *The Evolution of Educational Thought.* New York: Routledge, 1977.

Fetterman, D. M. "Empowerment Evaluation." *Evaluation Practice,* 1994, *15* (1), 1–15.

Franke-Wikberg, S., and Lundgren, U. P. *Att värdera utbildning* [To evaluate education]. Stockholm: Wahlström & Widstrand, 1979.

Freeman, H. E., and Rossi, P. H. *Evaluation: A Systematic Approach.* (5th ed.) Thousand Oaks, Calif.: Sage, 1993.

Goodson, I. *The Making of the Curriculum.* Bristol, Pa.: Falmer Press, 1988.

Guba, E. G. (ed.). *The Paradigm Dialog.* Thousand Oaks, Calif.: Sage, 1990.

Haug, P. *Educational Reform by Experiment.* Stockholm: HLS Förlag, 1992.

Haug, P. "The Evaluation of Governmental Reforms." *Evaluation,* 1996, 2 (4), 417–430.

Haug, P. "Theory-Oriented Evaluation of Reforms." *Nordisk Pedagogik,* 1997, 2 (17), 66–76.

House, E. R. "Integrating the Quantitative and Qualitative." In C. S. Reichardt and S. E. Rallis (eds.), *The Qualitative-Quantitative Debate: New Perspectives.* New Directions for Program Evaluation, no. 61. San Francisco: Jossey-Bass, 1994.

House, E. R. "Putting Things Together Coherently: Logic and Justice." In D. M. Fournier (ed.), *Reasoning in Evaluation: Inferential Links and Leaps.* New Directions for Program Evaluation, no. 68. San Francisco: Jossey-Bass, 1995.

Karlsen, G. E. *Desentralisert skoleutvikling* [Decentralized development of school]. Oslo: adNotam, 1993.

Lindensjö, B., and Lundgren, U. P. *Politisk styrning och utbildningsreformer* [Political government and educational reforms]. Stockholm: Liber, 1986.

Lundgren, U. P. "Using Evaluation to Monitor Educational Change." D. L. Grant (ed.), *Monitoring Ongoing Programs.* New Directions for Program Evaluation, no. 3. San Francisco: Jossey-Bass, 1978.

March, J. G., and Olsen, J. P. *Rediscovering the Institutions.* New York: Free Press, 1989.

Norwegian Official Information. *Maktutredningen. Sluttrapport* [End report from the project. Distribution of power]. Oslo: Norwegian Official Information, 1982.

Patton, M. Q. "The Evaluator's Responsibility for Utilization." *Evaluation Practice,* 1988a, *9* (2).

Patton, M. Q. "How Primary Is Your Identity as an Evaluator?" *Evaluation Practice,* 1988b, *9* (2).

Sabatier, P. A. "What Can We Learn from Implementation Research?" In F. Kaufmann, G. Majone, V. Ostrom, and W. Wirth (eds.), *Guidance, Control, and Evaluation in the Public Sector.* Berlin: de Gruyter, 1986.

Sabatier, P. A. "Knowledge, Policy-Oriented Learning, and Policy Change." *Knowledge Creation, Diffusion, Utilization,* 1987, *8* (4), 649–692.

Schwandt, T. A. "Evaluation as Practical Hermeneutics." *Evaluation,* 1997, *3* (1), 69–83.

Scriven, M. *Evaluation Thesaurus.* (4th ed.) Thousand Oaks, Calif.: Sage, 1991.

Scriven, M. *Hard-Won Lessons in Program Evaluation.* New Directions for Program Evaluation, no. 58. San Francisco: Jossey-Bass, 1993.

Scriven, M. "The Logic of Evaluation and Evaluation Practice." In D. M. Fournier (ed.), *Rea-*

soning in Evaluation: Inferential Links and Leaps. New Directions for Program Evaluation, no. 68. San Francisco: Jossey-Bass, 1995.

Shadish, W. R., Jr., Cook, T. D., and Leviton, L. C. *Foundations of Program Evaluation: Theories of Practice.* Thousand Oaks, Calif.: Sage, 1991.

Smith, M. F. "Evaluation Utilization Revisited." J. A. McLaughlin, L. J. Weber, R. W. Covert, and R. B. Ingle (eds.), *Evaluation Utilization,* New Directions for Program Evaluation, no. 39. San Francisco: Jossey-Bass, 1988.

Smith, N. "The Influence of Societal Games on the Methodology of Evaluation Inquiry." In D. M. Fournier (ed.), *Reasoning in Evaluation: Inferential Links and Leaps.* New Directions for Program Evaluation, no. 68. San Francisco: Jossey-Bass, 1995.

Stake, R. *Quieting Reform.* Urbana: University of Illinois Press, 1986.

Weiler, H. N. "Politics of Educational Reform." In R. L. Merritt and A. J. Merritt (eds.), *Innovation in the Public Sector.* Thousand Oaks, Calif.: Sage, 1985.

Weiler, H. N. "Why Reforms Fail the Politics of Education in France and the Federal Republic of Germany." *Journal of Curriculum Studies,* 1989, p. 421.

Weiss, C. H. "The Politicization of Evaluation Research." *Journal of Social Issues,* 1970, 26 (4), 57–68.

Weiss, C. H. "Evaluation for Decisions: Is Anybody There? Does Anybody Care?" *Evaluation Practice,* 1988a, 9 (1), 5–19.

Weiss, C. H. "If Program Decisions Hinged Only on Information: A Response to Patton." *Evaluation Practice,* 1988b, 9 (2), 87–92.

PEDER HAUG *is associate professor in pedagogy at Volda University College, School of Education, in Volda, Norway, and research coordinator in the Research Council of Norway.*

Evaluation practice conceived in terms of a Socratic dialogue offers a
particular kind of benefit for evaluation in a Swedish political context.

Socratic Dialogue in the Swedish
Political Context

Ove Karlsson

In Sweden during the last decades, new forms of social steering have been
introduced that emphasize political goals and decentralization. This has raised
the demand for evaluation as a tool for decision making. Increasingly, it has
also led politicians and other stakeholder groups to demand a voice in evaluation.

In this situation, critical questions emerge: How should the evaluation
claims from unfairly treated groups be incorporated? How should issues and
concerns be selected as the basis for deciding what should be evaluated? How
should criteria for the evaluation itself be chosen? These questions put evaluation practice in the middle of a value-laden discourse and raise the issue of
what strategies the evaluator should choose in order to handle evaluation in
this political context.

In this chapter, I first sketch how evaluation has developed in a Swedish
political context and then explore strategies for the future development of evaluation in this context. Finally, I suggest that a Socratic type of critical dialogue
could prove fruitful. The perspective on evaluation that I present mainly comes
from the field of education, but the developments discussed here are in many
ways parallel to perceptions of evaluation in other parts of the public sector.

Evaluation in a Swedish Political Context

It is no exaggeration to say that during the last ten years, evaluation has
become one of the hottest issues and concepts in politics and in the Swedish
public sector. The Swedish term for evaluation, *utvärdering,* is rather new to
the Swedish language. Swedish dictionaries mentioned it for the first time in

NEW DIRECTIONS FOR EVALUATION, no. 77, Spring 1998 © Jossey-Bass Publishers the early 1970s (Vedung, 1992b). That does not mean, however, that the activity is new, especially not in assessments of education.

School inspections, established in the late nineteenth century to control content and quality in the educational system, could be seen as a form of evaluation activity. The inspectors carried out observations in different schools and reported to the central government. They did what today we might call an "expert evaluation," using participatory observation to collect data (Franke-Wikberg and Lundgren, 1980).

Like other Western countries during the 1950s, Sweden went through a period of rapid industrialization. That led, among other things, to greater claims on the functions and tasks of the educational system. The strategy of evaluation, which was established in this period, used educational testing to choose the right student for the right place in the system.

As education expanded in the 1960s, a need developed for models of planning, both for organizing schools and for improving teachers' performance. The aim was to educate as many people as possible in the shortest time. There was a need for information that would allow efficient organization of the system and that would facilitate accurate estimates of optimal capacity. In this situation, the demand for evaluation increased, especially in the form of measuring how many students passed through the system (Lander, 1987).

During this period of expansion, educational technology flourished, and a technological view of evaluation dominated the designs that were used to measure how the educational system was working. Education was seen as a "pipeline," to use a metaphor from House (1983). Education and evaluation enterprises were based on a firm belief in the possibility of planning and steering the educational system in a rational way. As Franke-Wikberg (1990) puts it, "The evaluation was often carried out in order to provide answers to questions of efficiency, effectiveness and productivity." Furthermore, "The goals were described and broken down to measurable entities that were addressed through test specific knowledge and abilities" (p. 161).

This situation began to change in the late 1970s, however, when fewer students pursued higher education. This caused a competitive situation between different educational programs, and the interest in evaluation became directed toward quality issues and program evaluation. During the 1960s, decision makers often wanted to use evaluation on the central level with the aim of controlling the system on the level below.

This notion of evaluation also became more problematic in the 1970s. As the reform strategy became bottom-up rather than top-down, and as decision makers tended toward decentralization, evaluation was used less to exercise control and more to change and develop the system. In place of a dominating, top-down approach, the emphasis shifted to development-directed evaluation, with dialogue and communication becoming important features. Evaluation ceased to be an activity that mostly studied education products or outputs and instead began to focus on greater complexities in the educational process.

Formative evaluation, knowledge for the purpose of improving the educational process, was desired. The evaluator's new role was to question and to analyze an issue rather than to try reducing the complexity to a level where precise questions received unequivocal answers (Kapborg, 1996; Franke-Wikberg, 1990, 1992b).

Changes in the Forms of Political Steering

These changes in how best to steer and evaluate education must be seen in light of two developments: the remodeling of the Swedish welfare system and the idea of democratically steering the state—notions that became more and more urgent in the 1980s. During this period, some of the basic beliefs about the Swedish political and state-supported welfare system came under attack from different interest groups and politicians who wanted a more restrictive policy. In Sweden, there is a strong belief in systematically collecting information and preparing before making a decision. The tradition is one of rigorous investigation. In this very rationalistic tradition, the state has established a governance system at the central and regional levels so that decisions about the allocation and use of social resources to solve social problems will be based on solid research.

Another important aspect of the Swedish tradition is the emphasis on cooperation and consensus. This has taken its administrative expression in the form of ad hoc commissions and a consultation procedure (remissystemet). Traditionally, every policy question of any significance has to be prepared in a commission before the government makes a decision. One example is the decision about a new national curriculum for the comprehensive school, and another example is the Swedish Board of Education's suggestion to implement a national program to evaluate education. The commissions often contain representatives of the political parties, trade unions, employers' associations, student organizations, teachers, consumers, environmental interest groups, and so on. After the commissions deliberate, their suggestion is sent to organized interest groups for their consideration and for the opportunity to have a say before a policy decision is made. This system of consultation means that commissions' reports are referred to a large number of interested parties—both public and private, official and nonofficial organizations, agencies, research bodies, and interested pressure groups—for consideration and written comment (Furubo and Sandahl, 1996; Richardson and Kindblad, 1983; Vedung, 1992a).

Through this large-scale exchange of written material, a program idea is "evaluated" before anyone decides to adopt it. After the decision, the program is supposed to be permanent. This situation differs from the United States, for example, where a program is often tested in a number of pilot cases and then evaluated. After that, it is viewed as an example for others to follow if they wish, rather than as a model that is obligatory for all.

In the 1980s, the strong belief in cooperation and consensus that had characterized the Swedish political context began to lose support. Central control in general, and from the state especially, experienced problems of authority. The state's authority to exercise central control was challenged. Politicians and managers on the municipal level wanted a greater voice in the politics of social programming. In addition, the belief in large-scale and general solutions decreased as a consequence of a growing pluralism (Olsen, 1991).

Decreasing support for large-scale and general solutions paralleled the growing dissatisfaction with the Swedish welfare system. Since the 1940s, the Swedish state has developed a social welfare program in which the state assumes total responsibility for the individual citizen (Pettersson, 1991). The state promises to ensure a person's well-being from "the lullaby to the grave," as Zetterberg (1997) puts it. The Swedish welfare doctrine, he says, implies that individuals should not depend on relatives, charity, or market forces for their social security. Public arrangements should be of such high quality that they alone would be sufficient.

Today, one can say that Sweden's comprehensive, central program for public welfare is in crisis. Rothstein (1994) points to several reasons that the once-successful Swedish general welfare policy was strongly challenged during the last decade:

Financial problems for the state

A view of the welfare policy as too generous and exploited by many groups in society who really do not need the state's support

A growing individualism that resists standardized solutions and the general character of the welfare system and prefers private solutions

A growing pessimism about the state's power to steer and control society, especially when it comes to the question of welfare policy

Furthermore, increasing numbers of groups are claiming that they have received unfair treatment and have demanded that the state compensate them for the effects of a worsening national economy. Antagonism has grown between different interest groups in society about how the welfare state should be shaped.

In this political climate of competing interests, it is becoming more difficult to obtain a clear and complete picture of a problem and of all the consequences of different choices before making a decision. The number of possible ways of solving social problems has increased, and no solution easily surfaces as the obviously best choice. Moreover, even when one solution appears to be popular, it is difficult to gain a political majority and consensus (Lindensjö and Lundgren, 1986). As a consequence, the Swedish administration is forced to produce more and more material to reflect many different perspectives on an issue. This amount of information works against the purpose of making things clear by suggesting many possible courses of action.

New Forms of Governance

The state's interest in steering (governing) education has been evident for many years in the Swedish history of education. In a democratic society, the state is supposed to secure certain democratic values as the basis of educational goals at all levels in the school system. That means that the state must be able to exercise power at the local level. An educated and enlightened local actor is expected to transform the production of knowledge and information from the central level into local goals, frames, and activities in the light of overarching central goals. These goals are shaped in the "formulation arena," that is, on the state level (Lindensjö and Lundgren, 1986). Wallin (1990) describes the process: "On the local level different parts of the [educational] system transform the goals into their own objectives and decide upon their means of reaching the objectives/goals. This defines 'the arena of realization.' Between the two arenas, i.e., levels of system, there is a problem of balance. There is no guarantee that activities on the local level do move in the direction set down in the goals" (p. 175).

This process can be described as an interaction between different interest groups—central politicians and decision makers who formulate overriding goals, and local politicians, teachers, and parents who must put those goals into practice. This power exercise takes place in a context of conflicts between the interest groups.

To handle these conflicting interests, politicians and administrators can use different steering forms or strategies to exercise their political power (Gruber, 1987). According to Pettersson and Wallin (1995), two main forms can be identified: (1) direct and reactive forms, such as the budget, laws, regulations, control, and inspections and (2) indirect forms and information steering, such as further education, job training, as well as support for local development work, evaluation, and research.

Direct steering means, for example, establishing principles of economic distribution or legislation that ordain what to do. Setting national goals for a curriculum and criteria for performance evaluation are examples of direct steering. Reactive steering—for example, inspections and control—is a monitoring activity directed at certain parts of the school system to check what is or is not done.

During the last decade, the steering at different levels in the Swedish public sector has leaned toward more indirect and informative forms. Indirect steering includes further training for teachers or principals to develop their competence. It also includes providing scholarships and different kinds of support for the development of the local school. Informative steering includes knowledge received through assessment, evaluation, research, and documentation.

Steering has also become more decentralized. This movement can be interpreted as one way of solving the problem of running a welfare state in an environment that has changed from consensus to conflict. At the same time, the decentralization of the educational system highlights the question of how much political and professional power there should be over education, as well as the matter of balancing power at the central and local levels (Lundgren, 1990; Vedung, 1997).

In the Swedish political context today, the exercise of power at the central level to secure basic values in a democratic society no longer can be done with a direct steering model. The state's steering activities must be done in more indirect forms. Although there are fewer possibilities for the state to steer the educational system directly, however, the politicians still want to know how the schools perform and develop and what results they produce.

In this context of decentralization and economic cutbacks in the public sector, evaluation has become a very important steering instrument for decision makers, just as it is for those in public administration, such as professionals and managers. Decision makers will use evaluations to legitimize their cutbacks of programs; public administrators will use evaluations to describe and defend their performance and demonstrate that they can achieve good results. At the same time, decentralization has created more room for local actors and interest groups to have an impact on what to do, how to formulate educational goals, and what to evaluate.

In this new context of conflicts between different interest groups and levels in the educational system, there is a need for negotiations and dialogue between different stakeholder groups. Can established models of evaluation meet this new situation of conflict and the need for negotiation and dialogue between different stakeholder groups?

Current State of Evaluation

Evaluation is commissioned and financed by politicians and bureaucrats at the state level and by municipal officials at the local level. In Sweden, evaluation is primarily a public sector responsibility and undertaking. Traditionally, therefore, few evaluations have been performed by private evaluation firms or consultants, although this is becoming more common.

Evaluations of public policies and programs are conducted for the purpose of assessing both implementation and effects. Typically, the assessment of implementation focuses on questions of economy and effectiveness, and the assessment of effects is defined in terms of goal attainment. Evaluations that examine program context—that is, circumstances and conditions associated with program processes and outcomes—are not common. Both formative and summative evaluations are conducted for the usual purposes of fostering change and development or for achieving control and measuring results.

In the past three decades, evaluation practice has been characterized by an alternating emphasis. Evaluation in the 1970s and 1980s was generally more formative and oriented toward process, whereas evaluation in the 1990s is generally more summative and oriented toward products or results. Evaluation practice is also influenced by several developments in related fields, such as economics and policymaking. In the wake of an influential management philosophy introduced in the Swedish public sector, there has been a renewed emphasis on measurement-based evaluation. This kind of evaluation has a strong focus on quantitatively measuring aims that are often expressed in economic terms. "Accountability assessment" would be an accurate label for that reawakened tradition (Franke-Wikberg, 1990; Rombach and Sahlin-Andersson, 1995; Vedung, 1997).

There is also a growing interest in quality assurance, especially among politicians on the municipal level but lately also on the central (state) level. Quality is defined by means of quantitative indicators. Systems of quality assurance are implemented to maintain levels of performance. This movement in the public sector to measure quality reflects the importing of prepackaged instruments and scales used by private consultants in the business sector.

Along with these developments on the municipal level, there is growing evaluation activity on the state level with more explicit aims to exercise control. The broadly managed national evaluation of the school system in Sweden, which started in spring 1989, is an example of an evaluation ordered by the government to fill the need for information at the central state level. Criticism has been leveled against this form of evaluation for being too product centered, too extensive to be managed regularly, too measurement oriented, and too focused on results (output) instead of on the educational process. Critics of this state-level evaluation argue that evaluation ought to be more theory oriented and should aim not only at description but also at explanation. In addition, they advocate for evaluation that is "horizontal" rather than "vertical," meaning that the evaluation of certain part of a program should be carried out by those who are responsible for the program itself. In that way, the development of the program is given priority over the results.

Such criticisms of centralized evaluation exemplify the polarization of two perspectives on evaluation in the Swedish context. These criticisms can also be understood in light of the two forms of steering mentioned above—direct and indirect steering. One perspective on evaluation emphasizes the need for information to flow to the central level, where decision makers can determine priorities and judge the efficiency of state policy. The other perspective emphasizes that local actors should do evaluation themselves. In the first perspective, the basic motive is control. In the second, the basic motive is program development with local actors steering the project (Franke-Wikberg, 1989).

This short overview of evaluation's role in the Swedish political context cannot do justice to the complex development of evaluation in Sweden. What is obvious, however, is that the power of evaluation has increased in this context of change. Furthermore, evaluation activity gives stakeholders visibility. For them to be mentioned in the political debate, ideally in a positive way, is of great importance. When politicians engage in evaluation, it is a sign that they have noticed a program and will scrutinize it in order to determine its future. This can be a threat to the program, but it also gives the program workers a chance to market their case.

New Developments

Three developing lines of interest in the Swedish evaluation context affect the state of evaluation further. First, there is a movement toward internal evaluation in the public sector. Second, there are growing arguments for using a theory-directed approach (see Chapter One of this volume), which would yield a broader and more critical perspective on evaluation. Third, there is increasing support for stakeholder evaluation as a means of involving different interest groups (Bryk, 1983; Gold, 1981).

The movement toward more internal evaluation began during the 1980s, when different administrative units at the central and local levels started their own evaluation units. Some of this internal evaluation activity could be interpreted as an attempt by the authorities to do the following: legitimate their own enterprises by showing that they are doing evaluation, exercise their power by controlling performances, and build arguments to defend the enterprises against external critique. A problem to be aware of in this development is that it makes it harder for citizens to obtain information and to control the activities of public organizations. Therefore, there are solid grounds for examining this development critically. In the American context, this problem has been recognized by House (1986), who has warned that the critical metalevel examination of an evaluation's quality will be more difficult to perform when evaluation is done mostly as an internal affair without any public control and when data are not available for the public and professionals to examine. There is also a risk that being a employee biases the evaluator; in the worst cases, the evaluator may refrain from criticism so as not to jeopardize his or her own position (House, 1986, 1988; Sonnichsen, 1987, 1989).

The argument of Franke-Wikberg and Lundgren (1980) for theory-directed evaluation could partly be seen as a way to avoid the risks entailed in internal evaluation. Franke-Wikberg (1990) explains that the idea is "to formulate to yourself and to others a frame of reference related to the phenomenon evaluated, to indicate from what perspective the evaluation is conducted, to encircle the object of evaluation and to clarify the meaning attributed to this object by providing it with a context" (p. 162). She also gives three reasons for determining such a frame of reference. First, it directs the evaluator toward the information that is most important to collect. Second, it provides a frame of reference with which to interpret the information. Third, it gives an informative label to the evaluation that enables interested parties to judge its standpoint and worth.

Both the internal and theory-directed approaches have the potential to involve different stakeholders in an evaluation. That is not the explicit purpose of these models, however. Stakeholders are seen mainly as important sources of information. The models give no answer about how to involve stakeholder groups in a more active and equal role in the evaluation.

From that perspective, it is important to take a closer look at a third development that also has a critical potential—namely, the growing interest in stakeholder evaluation that has become apparent during the 1990s. This approach is an explicit attempt to achieve increased justice within the evaluation; it gives different interest groups opportunities to include their own questions. The stakeholder evaluation model could also be seen as an attempt to break the dominance of the one-sided situation in which a commission defines the evaluation's aims and content. Furthermore, stakeholder evaluation ties in well with the Swedish tradition of having different interest groups cooperate and negotiate before making a decision.

The stakeholder model can be seen as a challenge to the existing power structure. Through the stakeholder model, the current decision-making process can be ameliorated, especially by allowing certain underrepresented interest groups to have more influence in the decision-making process.

There are problems with this model, however. One criticism is that it leans heavily on a presumption of consensus between different stakeholder groups. Another criticism is that it is based on a somewhat naive vision of the importance of society's predominant power structures. That vision presupposes that each individual really has an equal opportunity to assert his or her own demands and interests (Weiss, 1983a, 1983b). The interest groups in the evaluation of public policy represent different domains within public activity (Salisbury, 1970; Wootton, 1985). Karlsson (1995) identifies four groups that constitute each of the domains: politicians, bureaucrats, professionals, and citizens (taxpayers, clients, and users). This subdivision makes it possible to analyze more closely the context of the evaluation and the relationships and conflicts that can develop between different interest groups. The representatives of various domains try to pin the blame for bad performances or results on domains other than their own. The professionals can be accused of advancing narrow self-interests. The management in the bureaucracy domain could be accused of poorly organizing and managing the program. Both can be accused of resisting change.

Many have pointed out that evaluation is strongly connected with politics (Chelimsky, 1987; Karlsson, 1996; Patton, 1988; Weiss, 1987, 1991; Palumbo, 1987; Vedung, 1997). As with other models, the stakeholder model can be seen as a way to legitimate political power. For example, if politicians want to protect a program from scrutiny, they can argue that the interest groups involved in the collaboration have already evaluated it. Because a strong emphasis on users exists in the stakeholder evaluation model, this argument will appear to have merit.

To these problems connected with the stakeholder evaluation model one could add the question of how the stakeholder groups can and should be identified. Another question is how the representatives for the groups can be chosen. A third is how the differences in power among stakeholder groups influence the evaluation. These questions put the spotlight on the evaluator's role. Should the evaluator strengthen the powerless stakeholder? How could such a decision be justified? How would such a standpoint affect other groups' confidence in the evaluation (Karlsson, 1990, 1995)?

Because of this context, it is important to create an evaluation strategy that gives stakeholders, especially those who lack power, more of a say in the evaluation. When attempting to handle an evaluation democratically and fairly, what can the evaluator do in this situation?

Descriptive and Prescriptive Strategies for a Conflict-Laden Situation

To select criteria and standards that will serve as the basis for judging program worth in an evaluation, taking into account the views of multiple stakeholders, one could describe all the different values involved. On the ground of moral pluralism, Shadish, Cook, and Leviton (1991) argue for this descriptive approach. They say that society is characterized by multiple value perspectives and that the evaluator has no good foundation on which to synthesize multiple points of view. An alternative to this pluralistic position is to formulate a more objective position by depending on a prescriptive theory, for example about what the program's needs are or what moral claims it is making or should make.

According to Scriven (1993, 1995), the evaluator must synthesize multiple points of view and multiple criteria into a summative judgment of a program's merit or worth. This does not mean that the evaluator's personal, subjective views determine the values or norms chosen; rather, Scriven argues for "objectivist" evaluation. What it does mean is that the evaluator is responsible for judging merit and worth; he or she should not leave this matter to others. The grounds for this judgment must be a theory of what needs the program seeks to fulfill. House (1990, 1991, 1995) considers that the use of formal philosophical theories, such as Rawls's (1971) theory of justice, can serve to inform and critique the basis for valuation.

Using a descriptive approach, an evaluator lists the values that stakeholders hold, determines the criteria they use in judging program worth, and investigates whether stakeholders think the program is good and what they think should be done to improve it. Using a prescriptive approach, the evaluator advocates the primacy of particular values—for example, Rawls's theory of justice or a theory of needs—which helps determine what is good or bad about a program.

Unlike prescriptive valuing, the descriptive approach does not argue that any particular values should have priority. Using a descriptive approach, the evaluator describes the program in terms of stakeholders' understandings. According to Shadish, Cook, and Leviton (1991), this approach identifies relevant stakeholders' values, uses these to construct criteria and standards, and gathers and reports evaluative data in terms of those criteria.

A crucial question here is how to determine the relevant stakeholders' values. This choice cannot be made in any neutral way. One also wonders whether the description of values is not more complicated than it seems when Shadish, Cook, and Leviton (1991) discuss it: "Descriptive values are easily constructed by contacting stakeholders; no special training in ethics is needed. All this makes descriptive valuing more practical than prescriptive valuing" (p. 49).

As House (1995) points out, "An evaluator constructing multiple synthe-ses of values and interests seems necessarily normative, not descriptive" (p. 44). Even when using a so-called descriptive approach to valuing, the evalua-tor must interpret who the stakeholders are and determine which values are the most relevant. This process must have at least two steps. First, the evalua-tor describes what he or she sees as the stakeholders' most relevant values. Then, the evaluator communicates these interpretations to the stakeholders. In this process, some of the values will presumably change, and a partly new collection of criteria will be formulated.

The evaluator plays an important role in this process and must be aware of his or her own perspective when describing different stakeholders' values and criteria. (Compare this with the theory-directed approach of Franke-Wikberg and Lundgren, 1980.) There are no "natural" or objective criteria that the eval-uator can simply describe or reflect as if he or she were a mirror. Instead of being a mirror reflecting the will of the stakeholders, the evaluator inevitably adds to the picture. When describing the values, criteria, and judgments made by different stakeholders, the evaluator gives priority to what to describe and should reflect on how this priority is established.

One argument against prescriptive ethics that Shadish, Cook, and Leviton (1991) put forward is that it involves trade-offs. For example, Rawls's theory of justice focuses on the material needs of the disadvantaged, which libertarians object might require them to sacrifice resources that their theory says they can keep (for example, giving up more or all of an inheritance to taxes). Any eval-uator advocating a particular ethic should outline such gains and losses and consider whether it is worth alienating stakeholders who may object to the losses.

One could ask whether a descriptive valuing approach must not also out-line gains and losses. A prescriptive approach squarely faces the issue of which values are chosen and why. A descriptive approach tends to sidestep or ignore this difficult question. The problem seems to be that a descriptive approach to valuing is viewed as nontheoretical, as something natural that does not have to be explained explicitly. But there is no neutral position from which the eval-uator can only register facts.

A shortcoming of the descriptive strategy is that it tends to reproduce existing conceptions and opinions in the framework of given goals, thereby limiting the possibility of generating new knowledge. The evaluation risks sim-ply sanctioning or legitimating existing points of views and does not encour-age a critical examination.

Using a prescriptive strategy, the evaluator not only describes multiple value positions but also seeks to synthesize them into a single statement of pro-gram merit or worth. The synthesis could involve general norms—for exam-ple, norms for social justice, equality, freedom, and so forth. A problem here is how to determine, for example, whether social justice should be placed before freedom. Even if this choice is made with defensible, good reasons, the question is whether the client will be interested in an evaluation in which the evaluator reserves the right to determine which criteria should be chosen.

Another way to tackle the problem would be for the evaluator to use such procedures as negotiations or dialogue between the interest groups in order to reach a decision about value (Guba and Lincoln, 1989; Nemo, 1995). The purpose of negotiating would be to recognize or admit that there is a problem and to seek a compromise between the judgments of different interest groups to avert further conflict (Strauss, 1979). A weakness of the negotiation model is that it can have a static effect on the evaluation's result. In a negotiation situation, groups have only a limited readiness to reconsider their positions; they give up their original arguments reluctantly. Negotiation also involves problems of power and resources. An alternative is to create a critical dialogue between evaluator and stakeholder in which they work together to scrutinize a program's merits and flaws.

Critical Dialogic Strategies for a Conflict-Laden Situation

A critical, dialogue-directed evaluation is Socratic. A Socratic dialogue is not primarily a matter of defending one's own beliefs while criticizing what others believe. Rather, dialogue is viewed as a process through which one gains clarity about one's own knowledge and ignorance, as well as about those of others. This is especially so when the knowledge is tied to the participants, as in the stakeholder evaluation. The aim of Socratic dialogue is to find the knowledge or insight that participants already have in some sense, although they do not know they have it. Reflection and dialogue make that knowledge accessible (Molander, 1990).

The aim of the critical examination is to gain practical and theoretical knowledge about how we ought to live and how the world is. In Molander's view, the dialogue should also express what human reason is and what the good life is. He argues that dialogue is necessary when the given framework—for example, research techniques and a conceptual framework—no longer suffice, or when one has to reflect upon what one knows and understands.

The Socratic dialogue generally focuses on one or a few important questions, such as, What is knowledge? or What is justice? Transformed into evaluation questions, these become, What have we learned from the evaluation, and what can we say about justice in this evaluation? The critical dialogue aims to develop a deeper understanding of what the program means for different stakeholders in terms of limitations and possibilities, especially for disadvantaged and unfairly treated groups in society. Through the dialogue, powerless and unjustly treated stakeholders are given a voice in what is evaluated and what criteria are to be used both to identify critical evaluation questions and to judge the program's value.

There are several different concepts of dialogue. Buber (1979), for example, identifies three types: technical dialogue, a debate, and genuine dialogue. Technical dialogue is a form of parallel monologues in which two or more people come together but talk to themselves without a genuine interest in what the other has to say. The debate is also a "false" dialogue. Various people state their opinions, theories, and reasons or evidence for their viewpoints. The communication often resembles that used in bargaining or negotiation. The aim is to decide how something is or should be (Gustavsson, 1996). In a genuine dialogue, however, an "I" and "you" are established in a mutual and reciprocal relationship. "I" enter into the dialogue to gain knowledge, and "you" do the same, thereby forming a "we" that can help us learn (Molander, 1990). That does not mean that the goal is to reach consensus between the participants. Neither is the dialogue merely limited to a discussion or exchange between participants. Instead, the participants try to attain intersubjectivity in different ways to understand a problem (Bjørklund, 1991).

Another dimension in the concept of dialogue could be described in terms of distance versus nearness. Buber (1970) presents a concept of dialogue that presupposes a close face-to-face relation, whereas Bakhtin (1981) and Ricoeur (1991) advance concepts of dialogue and communication that admit distance in time and space. In the latter view, the dialogue could take place between different groups and individuals and between different cultures and social groups over long periods of time.

A third issue in the concept of dialogue is that of conflict and consensus. Buber (1979) and Gadamer (1975) argue that the important elements in dialogue are listening and understanding. The goal is to come as close as possible to the other's point of view and to understand it from "the inside" (Gallagher, 1992; Weinsheimer, 1985, 1991). This signals a dialogue of reconciliation, one that does not necessarily strive for consensus but rather for intersubjective understanding.

Even within a dialogue of reconciliation, conflict and critical examination occur. But this should not be misunderstood as any kind of violence. Conflict and struggle can be compatible with both love and friendship. Gustavsson (1996) explains the difference between (1) struggle-based conflict that involves combat and ends with some defeat and (2) a dialogue-based conflict in which the participants cooperate and try to exchange ideas and viewpoints. In the Scandinavian tradition, this difference is known as *holmgång* versus *kretsgång*. In *holmgång*, one of the two combatants brandished his sword in his hand as the final conqueror. In *kretsgång*, the aim was not to destroy the other but to exchange experiences and to learn. This aim was important and had to be respected by all combatants.

I will now propose a concept of dialogue in the spirit of Socrates—a dialogue that is critical, conflict oriented, and not limited to face-to-face relations. This critical dialogue aims to have different groups and cultures exchange perspectives, knowledge, and opinions. To make this exchange a learning process, the participants must not avoid conflict and a critical examination.

Critical dialogue assumes that social change is both possible and desirable. Change is facilitated by a critical examination of circumstances that create injustice. To make it possible for minorities and groups in a weak social position to have a say in the evaluation, the evaluator must try to establish as much of a power-free dialogue as is possible between stakeholders.

This notion of a power-free dialogue between interest groups is associated with Habermas (1984), among others. He views power-free dialogue as noncoercive communication in which people use common sense and make democratic decisions that lead to consensus and truth: "It is assumed that the parties to his dialogue will consistently act in the discussion on purely rational grounds, avoiding all irrational influences" (Engdahl, 1991, pp. 46–47).

Habermas's theory of dialogue has been criticized on several grounds. For example, it assumes an ideal world in which there is no ruling elite. There is also an element of universalism in his model, in that the rules for argumentation are fixed, independent of the concrete situations and the people involved. There is a strong emphasis on having the participants achieve consensus about what goals to reach. With these criticisms in mind, it would be interesting and fruitful to think now about another perspective on dialogue.

Similar to my point of view, Welch (1990) and Benhabib (1994) regard the concept of dialogue more critically. From their perspective, the participants in a dialogue reach no agreement whatsoever, but they part as friends. As in *kretsgång,* dialogue has achieved something different—a comprehensive illumination of participants' own philosophies of life and personalities. The aim is not so much a matter of "developing" thought but of "breaking up" thought.

The critical dialogue in evaluation has the intention of understanding, of "seeing through" and critically examining in order to attain increased insight. Consequently, this kind of dialogue can be described as a meditative process in which the individual examines and verifies his or her own and others' perspectives and assumptions. All participants in the dialogue critique themselves and their own ideologies.

When talking about *a change in perspective,* I underline the difference between two interpretations of the term. In a weak interpretation, *a change in perspective* means seeing things from another point of view. A stronger interpretation refers to self-transformation. In the latter sense, this process involves an often painful transformation of one's view.

The main goal in critical dialogue is not to reach consensus (even if that could be the result). Rather, the primary goal is to reach greater insight and clarity about the foundations of one's own and others' judgments. Ideally, through this process, each party becomes enlightened and thus able to make more insightful and informed judgments and decisions. The participants become more fully aware of the limits of their own perspectives and of the difficulty of completely understanding how things really are.

An evaluator has at least two responsibilities in making a critical dialogue possible: to develop a theoretical perspective on the program and to cultivate a role as a critical inquirer. *Theoretical perspective* here does not refer to a complete model or explanation to be tested but rather to a framework that puts the object (program, policy, and so on) being evaluated in a historical and political context that can give new insights and views to the discussion and evaluation (Franke-Wikberg, 1992a).

Furthermore, the evaluator can emphasize that there are seldom simple answers or unambiguous results when one deals with qualified judgments, such as those that one finds when evaluating social and pedagogical activities. With such a theory-directed perspective, the evaluation process becomes not only a matter of putting together and describing interest groups' opinions and standpoints but also of developing a better theoretical understanding of the context of the program or policy being evaluated and the problems that could be connected with different parts of that context.

Conclusion

I have underlined the connections between the theory of evaluation and political and social changes in Swedish society. Because of increasing conflicts between different interest groups and a movement in the democratic steering system toward decentralization, evaluation has become an important activity for politicians and decision makers as they exercise power and seek to influence society.

In this situation, it is a challenge for evaluators to develop independent and critical evaluations that could not only answer questions for those in power but also address the needs of different stakeholders involved in the evaluation, especially those who lack power.

I have suggested that the evaluation process be reconceptualized in the spirit of a critical Socratic discourse. In this discourse, the evaluator acts as an interrogator who helps participants develop self-understanding and critical reflection. The strategy is not unproblematic. It demands that every interest group have the resources to participate. In addition, the Socratic discourse itself must be viewed critically. It presupposes a strong belief in rationality and a very authoritarian pedagogical discourse. Critics say that it overestimates the importance of rational thinking and underestimates concrete thinking and the importance of the emotional life for the intellectual. Socrates believed that a person who knows what is right will do the right thing and that self-knowledge is the path to all other knowledge.

I am not emphasizing this very rational and authoritarian part of the Socratic discourse so much as the dialectic method and the idea that greater knowledge and insight can be reached through reflection and critical dialogue and debate (Thesleff, 1990). Adler (1977, p. 190) describes this understanding of the Socratic method as "using questions to increase understanding in a primarily inductive and dialectical way."

In spite of the difficulties that characterize the approach, the strategy of critical dialogue could enhance the development of the stakeholder-oriented evaluation model in a political context. At the very least, it has relevance for the aspiration to develop the evaluation process in a democratic and fair way.

References

Adler, M. J. *Reforming Education: The Opening of the American Mind*. Old Tappan, N.J.: Macmillan, 1977.

Bakhtin, M. M. "Epic and Novel: Toward a Methodology for the Study of the Novel." In M. Holquist (ed.), *The Dialogic Imagination: Four Essays by M. M. Bakhtin*. Austin: University of Texas Press, 1981.

Benhabib, S. *Autonomi och gemenskap: Kommunikativ etik, feminism och postmodernism* [Situating the self: Gender, community, and postmodernism in contemporary ethics]. Göteborg, Sweden: Bokförlaget Daidalos AB, 1994.

Bjørklund, S. *Forskningsanknytning genom disputation* [To connect research through disputation]. Stockholm: Almqvist & Wiksell International, 1991.

Bryk, A. S. (ed.). *Stakeholder-Based Evaluation*. New Directions for Program Evaluation, no. 17. San Francisco: Jossey-Bass, 1983.

Buber, M. *I and Thou*. (W. Kaufman trans.). Edinburgh: T&T Clark, 1970.

Buber, M. *Between Man and Man*. London: Fount Paperback, 1979.

Chelimsky, E. "What Have We Learned About the Politics of Program Evaluation?" *Evaluation Practice*, 1987, *8* (1), 5–21.

Engdahl, H. "Dialogue and Enlightenment." In B. Göranzon and M. Florin (eds.), *Dialogue and Technology: Art and Knowledge*. New York: Springer-Verlag, 1991.

Franke-Wikberg, S. "The American Research on Educational Evaluation and the National Evaluation in Sweden." In M. Granheim, M. Kogan, and U. P. Lundgren (eds.), *Evaluation as Policymaking*. London: Kingsley, 1990.

Franke-Wikberg, S. "Profilen: Sigbrit Franke-Wikberg" [The Profile: Sigbrit Franke-Wikberg]. *Forskning om utbildning*, 1992a, *19* (3), 45–51.

Franke-Wikberg, S. *Utvärderingens mångfald. Några ledtrådar för vilsna utbildare* [The multiplicity of evaluation. Some clues for lost educators]. Stockholm: Universitets-och Högskoleämbetet, 1992b.

Franke-Wikberg, S. (ed.). *Skolan och utvärderingen* [The school and the evaluation]. Stockholm: HLS Förlag, 1989.

Franke-Wikberg, S., and Lundgren, U. P. *Att värdera undervisning, Del 1* [Evaluating education, Part One]. Stockholm: Wahlström & Widstrand, 1980.

Furubo, J.-E., and Sandahl, R. *Some Notes on Evaluation in Sweden*. Newsletter of the European Evaluation Society, Jan. 1996. (c/o Riksrevisionsverket, P.O. Box 4507–0, S10430 Stockholm, Sweden.)

Gadamer, H.-G. *Truth and Method*. New York: Continuum, 1975.

Gallagher, S. *Hermeneutics and Education*. Albany, N.Y.: SUNY Press, 1992.

Gold, N. *The Stakeholder Process in Educational Program Evaluation*. Washington, D.C.: National Institute of Education, 1981.

Gruber, J. E. *Controlling Bureaucracies: Dilemmas in Democratic Governance*. Berkeley: University of California Press, 1987.

Guba, E. G., and Lincoln, Y. S. *Fourth Generation Evaluation*. Thousand Oaks, Calif.: Sage, 1989.

Gustavsson, B. *Bildning I vår tid. Om bildningens möjligheter och villkor I det moderna samhället* [Education in our time. About the possibilities and conditions for education in modern society]. Stockholm: Wahlström & Widstrand, 1996.

Habermas, J. *The Theory of Communicative Action: Reason and the Rationalization of Society*. Boston: Beacon Press, 1984.

House, E. R. "How We Think About Evaluation." In E. R. House (ed.), *Philosophy of Evaluation*. New Directions for Program Evaluation, no. 19. San Francisco: Jossey-Bass, 1983.

House, E. R. "Internal Evaluation." *Evaluation Practice*, 1986, 7 (1), 63–64.

House, E. R. "Evaluating the FBI: A Response to Sonnichsen." *Evaluation Practice*, 1988, 9 (3), 43–46.

House, E. R. "Methodology and Justice." In K. A. Sirotnik (ed.), *Evaluation and Social Justice: Issues in Public Education.* New Directions for Program Evaluation, no. 45. San Francisco: Jossey-Bass, 1990.

House, E. R. "Evaluation and Social Justice: Where Are We?" In M. W. McLaughlin and D. C. Phillips (eds.), *Evaluation and Education: At Quarter Century.* Chicago: University of Chicago Press, 1991.

House, E. R. "Putting Things Together Coherently: Logic and Justice." In D. M. Fournier (ed.), *Reasoning in Evaluation: Inferential Links and Leaps.* New Directions for Program Evaluation, no. 68. San Francisco: Jossey-Bass, 1995.

Kapborg, I. "Evaluation of Swedish Nursing Education and Professional Practice." *Studies in Educational Sciences 4.* Stockholm: HLS-Förlag, 1996.

Karlsson, O. *Utvärdering av fritidsklubbar* [Evaluation of school-age child-care/youth clubs]. Eskilstuna, Sweden: Socialtjänsten, 1990.

Karlsson, O. *Att utvärdera-mot vad? Om kritierie problemet vid intressentutvärdering* [To evaluate—to what purpose? On the problem of criteria in interest evaluation]. Studies in Educational Sciences, no. 1. Stockholm: HLS Förlag, 1995.

Karlsson, O. "A Critical Dialogue in Evaluation: How Can the Interaction Between Evaluation and Politics Be Tackled?" *Evaluation,* 1996, *2* (4), 405–416.

Lander, R. *Utvärderingsforskning—till vilken nytta? Pedagogiska röster och två exempel från forskningsfältet skolutveckling* [Evaluation research—what good is it? Educational voices and two examples from the research field of school development]. Göteborg: Acta Universitatis Gothoburgensis, 1987.

Lindensjö, B., and Lundgren, U. P. "Att skilja det goda från det dåliga" [To separate the good from the bad]. In I. Palmlund (ed.), *Utvärdering av offentlig verksamhet* [Evaluation in the public sector]. Stockholm: Liber, 1986.

Lundgren, U. P. "Educational Policy-Making, Decentralisation, and Evaluation." In M. Granheim, M. Kogan, and U. P. Lundgren (eds.), *Evaluation as Policymaking.* London: Kingsley, 1990.

Molander, B. "Socratic Dialogue: On Dialogue and Discussion in the Formation of Knowledge." In B. Göranzon and M. Florin (eds.), *Artificial Intelligence, Culture and Language: On Education and Work.* New York: Springer-Verlag, 1990.

Nemo, D. *School-Based Evaluation: A Dialogue for School Improvement.* New York: Pergamon Press, 1995.

Olsen, P. *Svensk demokrati I förändring* [The change of Swedish democracy]. Helsingborg, Sweden: Carlssons Bokförlag, 1991.

Palumbo, D. J. (ed.). *The Politics of Program Evaluation.* Thousand Oaks, Calif.: Sage, 1987.

Patton, M. Q. "Politics and Evaluation." *Evaluation Practice,* 1988, *9* (1), 89–99.

Pettersson, O. "Democracy and Power in Sweden." *Scandinavian Political Studies,* 1991, *14* (2), 173–191.

Pettersson, S., and Wallin, E. "Utvärderingsmakt" [Power of evaluation]. In B. Rombach and K. Sahlin-Andersson (eds.), *Från sanningssökande till styrmedel. Moderna utvärderingar I offentlig sektor* [From a search for truth to a means of steering. Modern evaluation in the public sector]. Stockholm: Nerenius & Santérus Förlag, 1995.

Rawls, J. *A Theory of Justice.* Oxford: Oxford University Press, 1971.

Richardson, J., and Kindblad, B.-M. "Programme Evaluation and Effectiveness Auditing in Sweden: The Changing Swedish Policy Style." *Scandinavian Political Studies,* 1983, *6* (1), 75–98.

Ricoeur, P. "The Conflict of Interpretations: Debate with Hans-Georg Gadamer." In Mario J. Valdés (ed.), *A Ricoeur Reader: Reflection and Imagination.* New York: Harvester Wheatsheaf, 1991.

Rombach, B., and Sahlin-Andersson, K. (eds.). *Från sanningssökande till styrmedel. Moderna utvärderingar I offentlig sektor* [From a search for truth to a means of steering. Modern evaluation in the public sector]. Stockholm: Nerenius & Santérus Förlag, 1995.

Rothstein, B. *Vad bör staten göra? Om välfärdsstatens moraliska och politiska logik* [What can the state do? About the moral and political logic of the welfare state]. Stockholm: SNS Förlag, 1994.

Salisbury, R. H. *Interest Group Politics in America.* New York: HarperCollins, 1970.

Scriven, M. *Hard-Won Lessons in Program Evaluation.* New Directions for Program Evaluation, no. 58. San Francisco: Jossey-Bass, 1993.

Scriven, M. "The Logic of Evaluation and Evaluation Practice." In D. M. Fournier (ed.), *Reasoning in Evaluation: Inferential Links and Leaps.* New Directions for Program Evaluation, no. 68. San Francisco: Jossey-Bass, 1995.

Shadish, W. R., Jr., Cook, T. D., and Leviton, L. C. *Foundations of Program Evaluation: Theories of Practice.* Thousand Oaks, Calif.: Sage, 1991.

Sonnichsen, R. C. "An Internal Evaluator Responds to Ernest House's Views on Internal Evaluation." *Evaluation Practice,* 1987, *8* (4), 34–36.

Sonnichsen, R. C. "Open Letter to Ernest House." *Evaluation Practice,* 1989, *10* (3), 59–63.

Strauss, A. *Negotiations: Varieties, Contexts, Processes, and Social Order.* San Francisco: Jossey-Bass, 1979.

Taylor, A. E. *Sokrates* [Socrates]. Stockholm: Natur och Kultur, 1939.

Thesleff, H. *Platon* [Plato]. Göteborg, Sweden: Pegas, 1990.

Vedung, E. "Five Observations on Evaluation in Sweden." In J. Mayne, M. L. Bemelmans-Vides, J. Hudson, R. Conner, *Advancing Public Policy Evaluation: Learning from International Experiences.* New York: Elsevier Science, 1992a.

Vedung, E. *Utvärdering I politik och förvaltning* [Evaluation in politics and public administration]. Lund, Sweden: Stundentlitteratur, 1992b.

Vedung, E. *Public Policy and Program Evaluation.* New Brunswick, N.J.: Transaction Publishers, 1997.

Wallin, E. "Some Notes on a Norwegian Evaluation Programme." In M. Granheim, M. Kogan, and U. P. Lundgren (eds.), *Evaluation as Policymaking.* London: Kingsley, 1990.

Weinsheimer, J.-C. *Gadamer's Hermeneutics: A Reading of Truth and Method.* New Haven: Yale University Press, 1985.

Weinsheimer, J.-C. "Gadamer's Metaphorical Hermeneutics." In H. J. Silverman (ed.), *Gadamer and Hermeneutics.* New York: Routledge, 1991.

Weiss, C. H. "The Stakeholder Approach to Evaluation: Origins and Promise." In A. S. Bryk (ed.), *Stakeholder-Based Evaluation.* New Directions for Program Evaluation, no. 17. San Francisco: Jossey-Bass, 1983a.

Weiss, C. H. "Toward the Future of Stakeholder Approaches in Evaluation." In A. S. Bryk (ed.), *Stakeholder-Based Evaluation.* New Directions for Program Evaluation, no. 17. San Francisco: Jossey-Bass, 1983b.

Weiss, C. H. "Where Politics and Evaluation Research Meet." In D. J. Palumbo (ed.), *The Politics of Program Evaluation.* Thousand Oaks, Calif.: Sage, 1987.

Weiss, C. H. "Evaluation Research in the Political Context: Sixteen Years and Four Administrations Later." In M. W. McLaughlin and D. C. Phillips (eds.), *Evaluation and Education: At Quarter Century.* Chicago: University of Chicago Press, 1991.

Welch, S. D. *A Feminist Ethic of Risk.* Minneapolis: Augsburg Fortress, 1990.

Wootton, G. *Interest Groups: Policy and Politics in America.* Englewood Cliffs, N.J.: Prentice Hall, 1985.

Zetterberg, H. "Den falska bilden av svensk välfärd" [The false picture of Swedish welfare]. *Dagens Nyheter,* Jan. 5, 1997, p. 2.

OVE KARLSSON *is a member of the research team at the Centre of Welfare Research, University of Malardalen, in Eskilstuna/Västerås, Sweden. He has written extensively about the need for a more developed exploration of the role of values in evaluation, and he has also been involved in many projects, including evaluations of education and day care services and changes in the management of the public sector.*

The meaning of modernization as a strategy for reforming the Danish welfare state must be deconstructed in order to reveal a proper role for evaluation practice.

Evaluation as a Strategy of Modernization

Linda Andersen

> In general, I think it's a good idea to offer human service clients a wider influence on their lives, even though efficiency and rationality often accompanies these demands. But it is easier said than done. It requires many resources, time, and patience, not to mention specialized and professional expertise, to be part of fruitful dialogues and cooperation. Old habits and ideas are difficult to change. And these need to be worked over to facilitate further development.
> —Poul, human service employee

The practice of evaluation should be a natural element in the organizational, economic, and professional changes that constitute the aims of modernization in the Danish welfare state. Modernization is a development and economizing program designed to reform the welfare state. The idea is to make the welfare state more effective, efficient, and democratic in just one step. The public administration and politicians have masterminded this request or command to reform the state.

Modernization is an interesting experiment. Is it possible for a public administration to initiate change in societal, economic, and cultural processes by using traditional top-down command structures to ensure cooperation between state and county councils? Or do such ambitious changes require different methods and practices that involve personnel, clients, administrators, and politicians in new ways? What role and position do evaluation and education play in this development? Polemically speaking, one might ask whether it is possible for a top-down initiative to create bottom-up results.

NEW DIRECTIONS FOR EVALUATION, no. 77, Spring 1998 © Jossey-Bass Publishers

The introductory comment from a human service employee underlines how demanding and challenging democratic processes for change can be. They involve not only the professional responsibilities of employees but also their personalities and personal lives. Human development and change serve as the engine that drives the organizational changes at the core of modernization. It is difficult to imagine that sufficient change can be achieved solely by decrees from above. Change depends on small, lasting changes in the daily lives of institutions and in the everyday interactions between professionals and clients. It is precisely in the daily routines of institutions and professionals that an evaluation practice appears to be a highly appropriate strategy for modernization, both as a work style that reflects theory and methodology and as a research methodology in itself.

In this chapter, I seek to capture the discourses of modernization. What are modernization's goals and methods? Which symbols are central in its rhetoric? In what societal and cultural context is modernization embedded? Modernization is a demanding process of development and is therefore often based on supplementary education and a pedagogical development methodology. In this process, the practice and methodology of evaluation become important elements. How does evaluation represent results and methods of modernization, though, and how is the evaluator positioned?

I wish to draw the reader's attention to different currents in the discourse of modernization. The discourses of modernization are multiple, and the currents serve to illustrate various actors' assessments and understandings of the modernization project. These actors, all of whom have a part in the progress and results of modernization, are politicians and state administrations, leaders of institutions, and personnel and clients of human service programs. I stage different voices that I have identified through my research. Not all variations will be brought forth here, just as the underlying currents will not be thoroughly analyzed. That would not be possible in a chapter of this size. I hope, however, to leave the reader with an impression of the ambiguity and complexity created by the processes of modernization.

Background and Content of the Modernization Program

I was very excited the first time I heard that our institution was to become self-managed. I remember thinking that this was a great idea. Today, I am no longer so sure. Sometimes, when I am in a bad mood, I think that the difference is minimal. Other times, I am more optimistic. I participate in the management of the institution and take part in discussions about the budget and which activities we would like to have in our institution. At the same time, I think it is a good idea that we are given the right to decide what our own money should be spent on, even though I sometimes have long discussions with the staff when I spend too much money on cigarettes.

—Karen, resident of a mental institution

On the one hand, a local politician risks being stopped by citizens on the street, demanding that he account for the decisions made by one institution or another. At such a time, it is to your advantage to be able to say something that shows a certain amount of knowledge about the situation in question. On the other hand, we are no longer supposed to be so detail oriented. We are supposed to concentrate on the bigger picture. Thus, it is up to the institutions to [realize the framework that has been decided upon politically]. But I think that some politicians tend to be overly concerned with detailed administration. Perhaps there are those who won't or perhaps don't dare to let go of the control that strict and detailed political administration provides. However, in my opinion, this is founded on a great misunderstanding. Politicians are supposed to use their time and energy on more general political discussions. In what direction do we wish to see our society move? Which sociopolitical priorities should we be working for?

—Knud, local politician on the Health and Human Service Committee

The modernization of the Danish public sector has been the dominating rationale for development in the last decade. Clients, personnel, and politicians hold very different views of what this development entails, however. The one aspect that they probably share is that modernization is an unavoidable development. What does this somewhat broad and vague term actually cover, though? Simply speaking, the term signals that something outdated will be modernized, improved, and changed. The object of modernization is the welfare state—the products and services of the Danish human service and health system, educational system, and various public administrations. In this chapter, I will primarily focus on the attempts to modernize the field of human service within the public sector, although the actual modernization program spans much more than this one sector.

The modernization program arises from several sources. Partly, it stems from the public sector's excessive use of resources. Although the public sector has a large workforce, it commandeers a sizable part of the nation's annual appropriations. If that sector had continued to grow as it did in the 1970s and 1980s, the welfare state would have had to reserve too large a portion of state funds for the public sector. In the same period, citizens increasingly critiqued the public sector for its lack of service-mindedness and its slow and conservative work culture, among other things. The welfare state's work results did not seem to fulfill its mandate adequately. In the early 1980s, the Danish government passed a program to modernize the public sector (Pedersen, 1988).

The modernization program must therefore be understood in light of historic, societal, economic, and cultural changes that have taken place in Denmark since the 1970s. Ever since then, the program has been setting the agenda for organizational development in many public institutions (Dalsgaard and Jørgensen, 1994). Declarations of modernization and institutional development also have their counterparts in other European countries, although they have been characterized by significant national, cultural, and economic differences (Dalsgaard, 1992).

As the modernization program aims to reform the public sector and make it more efficient and democratic, the vocabulary of modernization includes terms such as *site-based management, decentralization, economic framework administration, client influence, debureaucratization, quality management,* and *interdisciplinary cooperation.* The program points to different tasks to be tackled in the process of changing the welfare state (Bentzon, 1988):

Decentralizing the responsibility for economic efficiency and personnel competence from a central state and county council level to the individual institution

Emphasizing market forces and increasing consumer choice, introducing the possibility of commercial enterprises in individual institutions

Improving service and creating rules that lead to increased service-mindedness

Using a more substantial and intensive program to train leaders and personnel

Using more new technology to improve efficiency and productivity

These changes involve economic, organizational, institutional, and cultural development processes, as well as subjective changes. In other words, modernization is a rather demanding and ambitious program. By way of illustration, I will show how these tasks apply to human service institutions.

Human service institutions now receive funds for site-based management. This means that personnel need increased formal competence in a number of areas, including transferring savings from year to year, deciding how to spend independent earnings, creating flexible budget divisions, and employing specialists in nontraditional ways (Andersen, 1992, 1996b). The framework of appropriation, which is politically decided, is to be negotiated between the institution's different parts: supervisors, personnel, and possibly clients. This means discussing and ranking the institution's operational costs and activities. Supervisors and personnel must organize the institution's treatment profile and use of methods and will be held responsible for adhering to the general guidelines as defined by administration and politicians.

The idea is for clients to have a far more active and decisive role in the institution. For example, they participate in client committees that routinely discuss activities and treatment programs. They also create programs that the institution should organize for particular clients, outlining specific developmental goals for those clients.

These changes require supplementary education and development projects so that personnel, supervisors, clients, administrators, and politicians can acquire this new routine. Finally, new technology also plays a role in the strategies for change, albeit a limited one. For example, an institution could make its bookkeeping more efficient if it used local and networked computers.

The Discourses of Modernization

> Public administration today has changed. It is no longer appropriate to issue decrees. Instead, as administrators, we are supposed to produce inspiring and summarized texts and information that make the client, personnel, and citizens think for themselves. The public administration should be a cocreator of public services. But we can't do it alone. The trick is to encourage the creation of ideas that are open to interpretation and that others may continue to develop. But it isn't always easy! The classic bureaucrat sometimes pops up to talk about rules and procedures and produces formal civil service language.
> —Peter, public servant

The modernization program spans a pragmatic, linguistic, and symbolic discourse (Andersen, 1996a). The pragmatic discourse points to concrete goals for development and work methods and defines some of the main actors in the desired organizational changes. The linguistic and symbolic discourses consist of language codes, argumentation chains, and symbols and concepts that the "text" of modernization includes or seeks to constitute.

The linguistic discourse concentrates on an optimistic and mobilizing tone of language and argumentation. Through this discourse, a new and modern genre of state administration texts and information is produced—the open, interpretable, and flexible public text. Counties, municipalities, and public servants are invited to interpret and implement the program's goals (Høyrup, 1988). At the same time, however, the program is not decisively and unequivocally important. Perhaps it is more precise to say that its meaning has a mobilizing, initiating, and inspiring nature. Far more important are the interpretation and practice that the implementing counties and institutions perform. It is on an everyday basis—in the counties and municipalities, as well as in institutions—that modernization is constructed.

Modernization therefore requires an administration in new clothes—such as described by Peter, the public servant above. Nowadays, employees in public administration should be consultants who advise and guide (Andersen, 1988). This change is not painless, however. An old professional identity confronts newer, vaguer, and more demanding identities. The public administration is no longer the sole proprietor of the public sector's development. The public administration must now change to allow for interpretation and reflections in contrast to the classic bureaucratic rational method of functioning according to rules. The public administration also becomes modernized in a polycentric manner, in which communicative, symbolic, and subjective competence make up the foundation. Thus, the contours of the administration in modernity is outlined (Andersen, 1995).

In the modernization text, concepts such as site-based management and democracy hold very distinct positions. These concepts appear to be decisive ideological and practical sources of inspiration for achieving the desired changes. This is true in written discourse, in which the concepts make up the cornerstones in the desired new reality.

They are also vital in a practical discourse; used in the everyday language of the county and institution, the concepts find meaning in reality. It can be argued that the program for modernization is nothing more than dead text that comes to life when it is interpreted and realized in the everyday actions and words of public institutions. On the one hand, the discourse then profits from a historic, social democratic Danish cultural heritage in which democracy, participation, and solidarity have been key concepts. On the other hand, it is evident that site-based management and democracy in modern society are no longer such unequivocal and firm concepts.

The concept of site-based management has changed in the grip of the pragmatic and management-oriented modernization discourse. Originally, it represented a critical ideological and liberating practice that would give people autonomy in managing their own and others' needs at work; this would also create solidarity (Schmid, 1993). In the program of modernization, the concept of site-based management has an instrumental, efficiency-oriented, management-like emphasis. In the critical and liberating context, site-based management aims at liberation from market forces. In the spirit of modernization, however, site-based management aims at involvement with market forces.

The meaning of a democratic practice is ambiguous, as well. Despite a common source, the Danish model of democracy includes several variations; the democracy can be representative, direct, participatory, consensual (among the elite), and corporate organizational. These varieties all create different practices. It is therefore important to know how the concept of democracy is being interpreted in a given context (Villadsen, 1992). It is quite probable that different actors—including politicians, civil servants, institution employees, and clients—will hold different interpretations of the concept. The program's positioning of concepts such as democracy and site-based management therefore opens up different local interpretations and practices. This space for interpretation needs to be reflected in an evaluation's context and choice of methodology.

Thus, the modernization program—and decentralized and local practice—has created an explosive cocktail that combines the democratic goals of participation and influence with the economic goals of rationality and efficiency. The discourse contains two ideological and practical universes in the context of modernizing and organizing. A philosophical, ethical, and pedagogical viewpoint is fused with productivity and with an administrative and management rationale. It becomes institutions' task and challenge to achieve the democratic ideals and treatment goals while using limited economic resources. Time will show whether this mix will be the most efficient and economically viable.

The processes of modernization therefore establish a number of paradoxes, all of which are intertwined in human service: economy versus human development, motivation versus compulsion, involvement versus distance, site-based management versus pseudodemocracy, efficiency-oriented quality control versus democratic and client-sensitive quality discussions, and overbureaucratization versus debureaucratization. In an evaluative context, these paradoxes must be represented. This calls for reflexive evaluative methodological designs that can identify subjective, social, and symbolic aspects of modernization.

Modernization and Modernity

Nowadays, it is quite difficult in human service to work based on developmental goals in general. Today, that is a question we seek to answer in close cooperation with the individual client. Or at least we attempt to do so. Sometimes, what is best for one resident is not good for another. The grand theory and goals don't really exist anymore. Things are both good and bad. It can be a bit confusing at times. And one starts to doubt one's professional assessments and knowledge. What are you supposed to think about the problems and lifestyles of other people? Sometimes, it is difficult enough to find one's own way.
—Ingrid, human service employee

The zeal to modernize is not the only development rationale that influences human service operations and the lives of employees and clients. Working with deadlocked and problem-filled lives is also influenced by other societal developments. As described by Ingrid, the employee above, the conditions in which human service employees work are undergoing fundamental changes. There used to be clear, normative, and professional regulations to indicate what was best for human service clients. Today, making such decisions is a much more relative project that fosters insecurity. Social work is not so clear-cut anymore. What is considered adequate development and assistance for problem families, young mothers, or the long-term unemployed no longer has a standard and unequivocal answer. Today, it is necessary to uncover and discover these answers in cooperation with clients. Only at that point can strategies and plans of action be formulated and, perhaps, be put into effect. There are no guarantees, however. Modern life has become relative, ambiguous, and unpredictable.

Theorists of modernity point to cultural liberation as a distinct feature of modern society. Former traditions and interpretations are no longer useful. Today, every person must contemplate and construct an individual life project. Modern life has become reflexive. Cultural liberation means that modern existence is centered around the individual's life project, which is predominantly characterized by a workable and can-do mentality (Ziehe and Stubenrauch, 1981; Ziehe, 1989).

Others speak of discontinuity as a unique characteristic of modernity. Modern social forms and institutions have changed. Today, time and space have become separate, allowing the individual to be liberated from local habits and practices. Hence, social conduct has changed to something that may be established across distance and time (Giddens, 1991). Postmodernists speak of the "death of the great stories." The grand ideas of liberating humanity, raising consciousness, and establishing critical societal systems appear to have collapsed and lost their importance. Whatever meaning and importance remain necessary must therefore be constructed locally and decentralized (Lyotard, 1984).

Hence, the program of modernization can be interpreted as a social administrative footprint of modernity. Modernization presupposes that a communicative and symbolic discourse will be established, one that will be creatively free rather than weighted down by tradition and habit, one that will be decentralized and ambiguous rather than centralized (Andersen, 1996a).

The processes of modernization therefore profit from such features of modernity as reflection, liberation, and decentering. The changes depend on the reflections and involvement of many actors. New organizational practice necessarily relies on a certain degree of liberation from cultural, economic, professional, and subjective habits, norms, and procedures.

The discourse of modernization is local and decentralized, because it fundamentally depends on the interpretations and realizations of local actors. On the other hand, there is a distinct and historical tendency to subject the local level to a central sociopolitical and goal-defined perspective. This will necessarily mean disciplining and controlling individual and local perspectives. For example, on a societal level, we have discussed and formulated a number of goals for how different people should be integrated into society. But how much do we actually know about how physically or mentally disabled individuals wish to live? Do they have the same ideas of a good life?

The cultural and subjective patterns of modernity are intertwined with everyday life in human service, thereby presenting multiple dilemmas for involved stakeholders, such as employees, clients and their families, politicians, and civil servants. Modernity establishes a set of paradoxes and contrasts in the daily practice of institutions. For example, ideas of liberation and consciousness-raising have strongly influenced the canon of social self-perception. Public treatment programs have often been marked by normativity and normality. In this respect, liberation and reflection provide an open space for different strategies for life and sketches of possible lives.

The same notion, however, also signals a painful and constricting recognition of the flimsiness of the concept of modernity. Societal and economic realities do not correspond with modernity's contentions of freedom of choice and life as a reflexive project. Individual staging is further eroded by overriding treatment goals and sociopolitics.

At the same time, another flaw in the analysis of modernity is evident, especially in human service. The seductive element of modernity is that everything can be shaped and altered—that the individual, regardless of gender, class, or social background, is not bound by a determined destiny. Modernity does not abolish the reality of society, though. Instead, it installs another distressing paradox for the individual, who can only dream of shaping a life. Perhaps this is why modernity makes such "bloody" phenomena as power and suppression, gender and class, invisible in its representation of modern society.

Modernization and Gender

The female competencies in the areas of communication, human relations work, intimacy, pleasure and consumption, and visualization and self-direction, have become strong elements in the actions of modernization and the modern demands for certain qualifications (Nielsen, 1995). Yet there is a distinct and disturbing absence of gender in the discourse of modernization. Gender, or even the category "women," appears rarely in dominant evaluation research about site-based management, which operates with a sexless, if not male, subject. Gender as a constituent and significant parameter is ignored.

This interpretation of reality is all the more problematic because the modernization of the Danish public sector is largely a matter of gender. The public sector's labor market is predominantly filled with women workers; they constitute 70 percent of the workforce in the counties. Given that modernization efforts are especially strongly linked to these parts of the public sector, modernization is embedded in the discourse of gender. Issues of identity and development of professions, the culture of the workplace, wage negotiations and standards, coalition policy and practice, and images and relations between users or consumers and professionals are all decisive parts of an attempt to understand the daily practice of modernization.

Apparently, women embody the relational, social, and human dimensions of modernity and modernization. Site-based management in the public sector delegates some of the powers and competence that formerly lay in the (typical male) hands of the top administrative civil servants and politicians. Modernization, then, delegates power and influence to the female level of the labor market. Although more men are entering human service, it is still a female domain. From one perspective, women represent—but they are not represented (L. Andersen, 1995).

Education and Evaluation as Strategies for Modernization

A pedagogical and developmental practice plays an important part in the program for modernization. Both in the program text and in the local and decentralized institutional practices, developmental work and supplementary education are important turning points. The discourse of modernization situates the practice of pedagogy and evaluation in a rather significant role. A long and varied pedagogical tradition exists, especially within human service. This tradition of participant-oriented educational progress is changed, however, in the discourse of modernization. Pedagogical methodology and evaluation are to be initiated from above. In a far more tangible and measurable fashion, they enter a greater and externally defined logic of modernization. Thus, the prerequisites for qualification are altered as well as the evaluation context.

On the drawing board, the goals of modernization present very demanding qualification requirements. The program focuses on participation and democracy and thus demands communicative competence. Modernization also demands an awareness of the larger context and a cross-institutional perspective in which the life history and treatment process of the individual client serve as a decisive center of focus. Decentralization presupposes insight into operational and administrative functioning, as well as into the interaction between the institution's information channels and organizational structure. The professional qualifications that the employee should meet highlight the need for continuous education in treatment competence with a greater focus on prevention and aftercare. Finally, personal characteristics such as autonomy, the ability to separate and to involve oneself in an appropriate balance, closeness, empathy, and respect are presupposed.

Thus, the qualification profile of modernization is similar to a societal development of qualifications, characterized by a strong focus on personal qualifications such as the abilities to solve problems, be flexible, and cooperate (Andersen and others, 1996). These qualifications are closely intertwined with individuals' personalities, and in their concrete form and management they are based on individual personality structure. In other words, modernity's focus on individuality and reflection has its counterpart in the development of qualifications and the demands of the labor market. Here, the program for modernization appears to fit into the public sector's interpretation of the impact of modernity.

The Rationality and Psychology of Modernization

> To be in a workplace that focuses on site-based management can be somewhat of a strain. Having everybody actively partake in all these decisions is sometimes overdone! On occasion, people are very influenced by what goes on, and this affects their daily work and cooperation between colleagues and residents. Moreover, leaders and politicians don't always keep their promises. This causes much anger and frustration, and many lose confidence that the ideas of democracy are to be taken seriously.
>
> —Birgitte, human service employee

> It is remarkable how the research field reacts to my presence. This is a common experience for me. Apparently, site-based management awakens many feelings and thoughts in many participants. It influences me, too, partly because I have my own stake in the idea of site-based management. I believe this is a challenging and meaningful development of human beings. Therefore, I would like to contribute with constructive suggestions. But I am not always in control of what happens. Sometimes I react impulsively and without closer consideration when

difficult situations occur in my research work. Several times, on my way home from fieldwork, I find myself thinking about what my childhood and youth have meant for my understanding of the problems I encounter through my research.
—Linda Andersen, researcher

The emotional and symbolic aspects of modernization, as illustrated in the above statements, are subjective undercurrents that influence and color many modernization processes in institutions. In those contexts, feelings and experiences are intensified and then affect behavior. As a result, the researcher must use both empathy and distance to achieve an analytical understanding of modernized institutional daily life.

Many modernization processes embrace two different but equally important dimensions: a conscious, rational dimension and an unconscious, emotional one (Andersen, 1996a, in press). When organizations confront employees with demands for development, change, and modernization, the employees often respond with ambivalence (Menzies Lyth, 1988, 1989; Ortmann, 1993; Wellendorf, 1986). Organizations tend to handle the demands of modernization in a manner that seeks to avoid emotional problem areas and reactions. Institutions and administrations tend to familiarize themselves with rational goal descriptions and goal implementations. Processes of modernization are often understood as an arena of rationality. The administrative and political forces of modernization are predominantly oriented toward a rational and instrumental practice, and they often fail to establish a more reflective space that accommodates ambivalent feelings and experiences. Employees' experiences of site-based management and democracy are probably influenced by their prior experiences of individualizing, gaining autonomy, and separating, which in turn influence their conscious or subconscious responses to the demands for development.

For example, I attended a sequence of meetings as I did fieldwork related to site-based management in a county. The meetings produced and activated conscious and unconscious experiences for the participants and for me. These experiences decisively affected the way the various actors responded to the goals and intentions of the site-based management and democratization experiment. An analysis of transference revealed that at the meetings, institutional personnel came to symbolize the ambivalence that site-based management activated. In my report of this work, I also attempted to describe my countertransference and the significance and influence it may have had on the research process and the interpretation.

At the same time, I expanded the framework of interpretation to include a theoretical discussion of how engaging in processes of site-based management and democracy seems to touch many people at the core. Depending on the nature of their psychodynamic childhood landscapes, people have a more or less conflictual relationship with site-based management. This psychodynamic stamp on individuals can influence, to varying degrees, how they handle the processes of site-based management and democracy. My interpretation was not embodied solely in an inner psychic reality, however; it also incorporated relevant social, economic, cultural, organizational, and professional aspects—in the form of a scenic analysis (Leithaüser and Volmerg, 1988; Lorenzer, 1986).

A Nonmonolithic and Reflexive Evaluation

These subjective and societal, real and symbolic interpretations are closely intertwined in an ethnographic, psychoanalytic, and action research approach in my analysis of modernization. Ethnography spans various traditions and interpretations in which the critical and liberating aspects of representation are stressed (Fetterman, 1984; Spindler and Spindler, 1992; Thomas, 1993). When ethnographic elements such as long-term fieldwork, cultural insight and interpretation, research positioning, and reflection are used to analyze the course of institutional modernization, the possibility of multiple stories is created. These stories are told in a way that grants actors such as human service consumers and employees a more visible role. Thus, a nonmonolithic and ambiguous representation can be created.

The discourse of modernization and modernity explodes the traditional linear evaluative process in which program goals are negotiated among stakeholders, formulated, implemented, and then evaluated. Various stakeholders and citizens wish to believe that this is the way to improve the welfare state and to create more democracy. In the highly rationalized tradition that dominates the evaluation of Danish modernization processes, a macroperspective on the program is widespread; a static, one-dimensional measurement of program effects is emphasized; gender is absent; and a one-sided focus on economic and administrative criteria at the expense of cultural, social, and professional results and processes is evident. All of this diminishes the ability to reflect the complexity of modernization (Andersen, 1996a). Through the process of traditional evaluation, a multifaceted reality is transformed and homogenized through a monolithic report with a homogeneous subject. Furthermore, these processes displace the unconscious in the construction of the evaluation report's empirical authority.

In contrast, the psychoanalytical viewpoint acknowledges the unconsciousness in science as in life. It emphasizes the ways in which the unconscious influences how people symbolize work and organizations. Unconscious processes also structure the researcher's data collection and relations between the researcher and research subjects (Hunt, 1989). The concepts of transference and countertransference are central to the application of psychoanalytical insight—both at the subjective and organizational levels (Devereux, 1967; Leithaüser and Volmerg, 1988; Wellendorf, 1986). The key is to establish a methodological framework that can represent social life in its multiplicity and depth. When transference and countertransference are used in research, they establish a path of knowledge that complements and deepens other forms of data collection. What is special about the path of knowledge followed by transference is that the researcher's awareness, intellect, and feelings transform the analytical processes. Thus, analyses of transference produce insight into the dynamics and content that are usually difficult to attain with other methods of data collection. Key psychoanalytical concepts are used as an analytical can opener for events and development traits in the processes of modernization.

A third methodological aspect involves participatory action research. This approach seeks to place research in the service of change and, thus, to create a distinct positioning between the researcher and participants (Argyris and Schön, 1991; Whyte, 1991). This research method reinterprets existing validation practice. Action research operates with a concept of validation that, first, involves researchers and practitioners in a process of hypothesis generation and testing, and second, incorporates reflection about demands for deeds and action (Argyris and Schön, 1991). Participatory action research decenters the researcher through the construction of authority, scientific authority, knowledge production, interpretive practice, and form of payment (Andersen, 1996a). On the one hand, this is one of the strengths of the ideological and methodological foundation of action research. On the other hand, this underemphasizes the methodological pitfalls that the researcher's authority and influence create, despite her desire for decentering. In practice, action research has a tendency to oversimplify the complex power relationships, the right to interpret, and the knowledge that the researcher always brings with her.

Conclusion

Different questions and stories come forward in an analysis that is neither fixated nor finished. Do processes of modernization have a discourse that instills discipline, liberates, or decenters? Does modernization have a feminine trait, or should we speak of various subjective and symbolic traits that differ by gender, culture, ethnicity, age, and profession? Is the researcher's position in evaluation that of a prism, transfer filter, cointerpreter, guarantor of action, modernist, facilitator, educator, observer, or storyteller?

Often, the evaluator's position periodically alternates between omnipotence and powerlessness. It shifts back and forth from unconscious and conscious motives and acts, on the one hand, to unintentional and calculated incidents and considerations, on the other hand. I think evaluators have a tendency to exaggerate the meaning of rationality. We underestimate and sometimes even neglect the impact of emotional and irrational motives, instead seeking and constructing rationality as the queen of science. The emotional drive behind our choice of research methods, theory, and interpretations is a fact that we underestimate or ignore too often. Rationality has a tendency to dominate at the expense of reflexivity.

As evaluators and researchers, we should recognize that we drift among different discourses during the evaluative process. We position ourselves in relation to stakeholders and circumstances, and we are also positioned by them. The most reasonable thing to do, then, is probably to feel and reflect—and write!

References

Andersen, L. *Styre eller styres* [To be controlled or to be in control: An evaluation of a three-year experiment with self-management in the county of Roskilde]. Roskilde, Denmark: Adult Education Research Group, Roskilde University, 1992.

Andersen, L. "Voices from the Borderland: Reflections on Power, Gender, and Action Within the Postmodern Human Service." Paper presented at the International Evaluation Conference, Vancouver, Canada, Nov. 1995.

Andersen, L. *Bag facaden* [Under the surface: Subjective and symbolic dynamics in the modernization of human service institutions]. Roskilde, Denmark: Adult Education Research Group, Roskilde University, 1996a.

Andersen, L. "A Voice of Your Own: An Educational Ethnography About Human Service in Denmark." In P. Rasmussen and H. Salling Olesen (eds.), *Theoretical Issues in Adult Education*. Roskilde, Denmark: Roskilde University, 1996b.

Andersen, L. "When the Unconscious Joins the Game: An Ethnographic and Psychoanalytic Evaluation." In Y. Lincoln and M. Levin (eds.), *Evaluation for Social Change*. Thousand Oaks, Calif.: Sage, in press.

Andersen, M. M. "Administrationspolitikkens nyorientering—et erfaringsbaseret syn på ændringer I organisation og ledelse" [The reorientation of administrative policy—An experience-based view of changes in organization and management]. In K. H. Bentzon (ed.), *Fra vækst til omstilling—moderniseringen af den offentlige sektor* [From growth to reorganizing—Modernizing the public sector]. Copenhagen: Nyt fra Samfundsvidenskaberne, 1988.

Andersen, N. Å. *Selvskabt forvaltning—forvaltningspolitikkens og centralforvaltningens udvikling I Danmark fra 1900–1994* [Self-made administration—The development of the administrative policy and the administration in Denmark, 1900–1994]. Copenhagen: Nyt fra samfundsvidenskaberne, 1995.

Andersen, V., Illeris, K., Kjœrsgaard, C., Larsen, K., Olesen, H. S., and Ulriksen, L. *General Qualification*. Roskilde, Denmark: Adult Education Research Group, Roskilde University, 1996.

Argyris, C., and Schön, D. A. "Participatory Action Research and Action Science Compared: A Commentary." In W. F. Whyte (ed.), *Participatory Action Research*. Thousand Oaks, Calif.: Sage, 1991.

Bentzon, K. H. "Forvaltningsreformer I den offentlige sektor" [Administrative reforms in the public sector]. In K. H. Bentzon (ed.), *Fra vækst til omstilling—moderniseringen af den offentlige sektor* [From growth to reorganizing—Modernizing the public sector]. Copenhagen: Nyt fra Samfundsvidenskaberne, 1988.

Dalsgaard, L. *Modernisering som institutionspolitik—Erfaringer fra 1980'er-udviklinger I England, USA, Vesttyskland og Frankrig* [Modernization as institutional policy—Experiences of development in the 1980s in England, the U.S.A., Germany, and France]. Aalborg, Denmark: Department of Economy, Policy, and Administration, Aalborg University, 1992.

Dalsgaard, L., and Jørgensen, H. *Det offentlige—sektorens og de ansattes værdier og værdighed* [The public—Values and dignity of the sector and personnel]. Copenhagen: Organization of Danish Lawyers and Economists (DJØF), 1994.

Devereux, G. *From Anxiety to Method in the Behavioral Sciences*. Paris: Mouton, 1967.

Fetterman, D. M. *Ethnography in Educational Evaluation*. Thousand Oaks, Calif.: Sage, 1984.

Giddens, A. *Modernity and Self-Identity: Self and Society in the Late Modern Age*. Stanford, Calif.: Stanford University Press, 1991.

Høyrup, M. "Om sprogbrug og holdning I moderniseringsprogrammet" [Language and attitudes in the modernization program]. In K. H. Bentzon (ed.), *Fra vækst til omstilling—moderniseringen af den offentlige sektor* [From growth to reorganizing—Modernizing the public sector]. Copenhagen: Nyt fra Samfundsvidenskaberne, 1988.

Hunt, J. *Psychoanalytic Aspects of Fieldwork*. Thousand Oaks, Calif.: Sage, 1989.

Leithäuser, T., and Volmerg, B. *Psychoanalyse in der Socialforschung. Eine Einführung am Beispiel einer Socialpsychologie der Arbeit* [Psychoanalysis in social research. An introduction to the social psychology of work]. West Germany: Verlag, 1988.

Lorenzer, A. "Tiefenhermeneutische Kulturanalyse" [The hermeneutic cultural analysis]. In A. Lorenzer (ed.), *Kultur-Analysen* [The cultural analysis]. Frankfurt: Fischer, 1986.

Lyotard, J. *The Postmodern Condition: A Report on Knowledge.* Minneapolis: University of Minnesota Press, 1984.

Menzies Lyth, I. *Containing Anxiety in Institutions.* London: Free Association Books, 1988.

Menzies Lyth, I. *The Dynamics of the Social.* London: Free Association Books, 1989.

Nielsen, H. B. "Kjønn som irritasjonsmoment I det moderne" [Gender as a source of irritation in modernity]. *Grus,* 1995, 47.

Ortmann, G. "Organisation und Psyche" [Organization and psyche]. In B. Volmberg, T. Leithäuser, O. Neuberger, G. Ortmann, and B. Sievers (eds.), *Nach allen regeln der kunst. Macht und Geschlecht in Organisationen* [The rules of the game. Power and gender in organization]. Freiburg, Germany: Kore, 1993.

Pedersen, J. "Fra bueraukrati til servicevirksomhed: En analyse af intentionerne bag moderniseringsprogrammet" [From bureaucracy to service business: An analysis of the intentions of the modernization program]. In K. H. Bentzon (ed.), *Fra vækst til omstilling—moderniseringen af den offentlige sektor* [From growth to reorganizing—Modernizing the public sector]. Copenhagen: Nyt fra Samfundsvidenskaberne, 1988.

Schmid, H. "Selvforvaltning I arbejdslivet" [Site-based management in working life]. In K. Bregn and H. Hvid (eds.), *Arbejdsliv I Skandivavien-brud og bevægelse* [Working life in Scandinavia—Breaches and movements]. Copenhagen: Forlaget Sociologi, 1993.

Spindler, G., and Spindler, L. "Cultural Process and Ethnography: An Anthropological Perspective." In M. D. LeCompte, W. L. Millroy, and J. Preissle (eds.), *The Handbook of Qualitative Research in Education.* Orlando, Fla.: Academic Press, 1992.

Thomas, J. *Doing Critical Ethnography.* Thousand Oaks, Calif.: Sage, 1993.

Villadsen, S. "Det deregulerede demokrati-det nye højres kritik af velfærdsstatens demokratiske institutioner" [The deregulated democracy—The new conservative's criticism of the democratic public institutions]. In S. Villadsen (ed.), *Demokrati? Moderniseringspolitikkens betydning for det danske demokrati* [Democracy? The policy of modernization and its importance for the Danish democracy]. Copenhagen: Forlaget Samfundsøkonomi, 1992.

Wellendorf, F. "Supervision als Institutionsanalyse" [Supervision as institutional analysis]. In H. Pühl and W. Schmidbauer (eds.), *Supervision und Psychoanalyse-Selbstreflexion der helfenden Berufe* [Supervision and psychoanalysis—Self-reflexivity in the helping professions]. Frankfurt: Fischer Taschenbuch Verlag, 1986.

Whyte, W. F. "Comparing PAR and Action Science." In W. F. Whyte (ed.), *Participatory Action Research.* Thousand Oaks, Calif.: Sage, 1991.

Ziehe, T. *Ambivalenser og mangfoldighed* [Ambivalence and multiplicity]. Copenhagen: Politisk Revy, 1989.

Ziehe, T., and Stubenrauch, H. *Plädoyer für Ungevöhnliches Lernen: Ideen zur Jugendsituation* [Speech for unusual learning processes: Ideas about youth]. Hamburg: Rowohlt Taschenbuch Verlag, 1981.

LINDA ANDERSEN is assistant professor in the Department of Educational Studies at Roskilde University in Denmark and is a practicing psychoanalyst.

The development of and prospects for Danish evaluation practice are best understood in light of an examination of two cultures of Danish social science.

Evaluation Research and Sociology in Denmark: A Tale of Two Cultures

Finn Hansson

> There seems then to be no place where the cultures meet. I am not going to waste time saying that this is a pity. It is much worse than that.
> —C. P. Snow ([1963] 1993)

"It is dangerous to have two cultures which can't or don't communicate," remarks C. P. Snow in *The Two Cultures,* his famous book on the two cultures in science. This powerful concept of two differentiated and very distant cultures of science—a natural, technical culture with a focus on scientific tools and procedures and a humanistic, social culture with a more hermeneutic, interpretive understanding of science—has in recent years been used in policy analysis and social science to characterize distinct methodological communities. In this chapter, I will use the concept of two cultures to analyze the differences and conflicts in the history of Danish sociology and the implications for the development of evaluation research.

Evaluation research in Denmark, as in most other Western European countries, draws on many of the social sciences, but influences from sociology and especially quantitative methodology seem to be most important. At the very least, evaluation research and sociology are interrelated and exhibit partly parallel development in Denmark.

The conflict-ridden history of Danish sociology (Andersen, Blegvad, and Blegvad, 1994; Boje and Hort, 1993; Hansson and Nielsen, 1996) reflects two cultures—one of an applied, empirical sociology and one of a university sociology that promotes a more theoretical and sometimes critical or radical sociology. A major difference between the two cultures is in scientific organization. From the beginning, applied sociology in Denmark was institutionalized as a modern administrative organization, not as a research community. It was inspired by the organizational and technical apparatuses used to collect and analyze social survey data; these apparatuses were developed in the late 1940s in the United States. University sociology, on the other hand, was organized according to the classical European university tradition of independence in academic matters. The two cultures also differ in relation to users and the public. Applied sociology in Denmark has a direct relation to clients, quite often with a high degree of political dependence because the client is frequently the political or administrative system. In university sociology, research questions typically originate from discussions in international sociology and general sociological debates.

From the early days of Danish evaluation research, the majority of the research was more or less embedded in the culture and organization of applied social research. When evaluations of policies, programs, and projects became more prominent in the 1980s, most were performed by the same applied social research institutions that had dominated empirical social research since the 1960s. Evaluations of development aid started earlier and in other organizational settings but were also dominated by narrow, empirical types of evaluations (Rebien, 1996). In the late 1980s, another evaluation culture developed. Based on smaller and more loosely organized research groups at the universities and private consulting agencies, this culture was more concerned with qualitative, probing, and interactive evaluations.

In this chapter, I will show that there are recent tendencies in Danish evaluation research and sociology toward integrating the two cultures. This trend is partly driven by the blunt failure of the classical interventionist model of social engineering in the face of changing functions and applications of social science in a modern society. On the other hand, the rapid development of internal evaluation—with its overwhelming use of empirical methodologies and quantification and its close relation to management and organizational interventions—could create a new dividing line in evaluation research.

Social Studies and Reforms

The Danish tradition of systematically collecting and using information about social problems and social affairs for political purposes goes back more than one hundred years. At the end of the last century, concerned social reformists collected statistics-based information in order to describe the burning social problems among the growing working class and to prepare the political background for social reforms. For example, Sørensen, a country doctor and social reformist, did several studies of the living conditions of farm and factory workers and their families, including information on work accidents, sickness, nutrition, and death. These studies had a great impact on the first laws on state unemployment insurance and sick insurance at the end of the 1800s (Sørensen, [1880] 1984). Around 1930, the systematic use of social statistics and information had grown so widespread that the ministry of social affairs inevitably established a social statistical consulting position.

World War II changed Danish society in many ways. The Social Democratic Party launched an ambitious welfare state program ("Denmark of the Future") with inspiration from the British Labour Party and the Beveridge Plan. This program, along with the planning efforts for the war economy, resulted in a more active state administration, as well as a political program. The political program was to change social policy from traditional ideas of poor relief to the welfare state (Thomas, 1977).

By the late 1950s, social statistics were an integral part of the formation of state policies. In 1958, the Danish National Institute for Social Research (SFI) was established as a research institution with close administrative, organizational, and financial links to the central administration. At the same time, it had no organized relations to academic sociology or university social research. The main political purpose behind the establishment of this new institution was to have a research agency close to the central administration and political decision makers. That way, SFI could produce statistics-based social information on the growing social and labor market problems that had beset Denmark as it moved from an agricultural society to an increasingly industrial, modernized, and urbanized one.

Yet, the use of this social information in policy planning and social reforms as a response to postwar social problems, and the subsequent evaluation of the reforms' efficiency and results, was not the concern of the new research institution. The administration and government evaluated the results of the reforms, using the traditional Danish negotiation system. Trade unions and employers' organizations, as well as other larger interest groups, therefore became involved both in the formulation of the problems and reforms and in their evaluation.

This policy of negotiating programs and the subsequent evaluations most clearly affected the labor market area, but many social policy reforms followed the same procedure after World War II brought a welfare state program to Denmark. This special Danish tradition of political negotiations for all major political reforms since the late 1920s explains a lot about why formal and independent evaluation studies were implemented so belatedly in Denmark (Albæk, 1996; Albæk and Winter, 1993).

The Start of Sociology and Applied Social Research

Sociology as an academic discipline was first established in Denmark in 1956 with the Institute of Sociology at the University of Copenhagen. The first professor was Kaare Svalastoga, a student of George Lundberg, who was a leading positivist in American postwar sociology (Bierstedt, 1981). Already at this early stage, it is possible to locate traces of the two cultures. Beginning early in the century, well before the establishment of the institute, and hence the establishment of sociology as a field in the university, sociology had been much discussed and debated in academic circles, especially among philosophers, reformist economists, and left-wing academics. The very clear, almost ideological, empiricist orientation of the new academic sociology marked a clear break from the more philosophical and social reformist orientation that existed before 1950. Furthermore, the institute did not at all relate to the debates within existing Continental sociological traditions, especially German and French ones (Agersnap, 1996; Andersson and Dabrowski, 1996).

A study using archive material (Andersson and Dabrowski, 1996) sheds some light on the background arguments and priorities in the political debate leading up to the independent establishment of SFI. Andersson and Dabrowski found no evidence that the economic and organizational gains of merging the two institutions, SFI and the Institute of Sociology, were ever seriously considered. An old cultural or traditional skepticism or suspicion toward academics and university research, especially in the social sciences, prevailed in Danish political life at the time. This was especially true in the labor movement and the Social Democratic Party, which had mainly seen academic professions as representing and supporting their political opponents. Part of this development is more general and rather widespread, as Porter (1995) reported in his study of the relations between science, experts, and public life:

> It is no accident that the move toward the almost universal quantification of social and applied disciplines was led by the United States, and succeeded most fully there. The push for rigor in the disciplines derived in part from the same distrust of unarticulated expert knowledge and the same suspicion of arbitrariness and discretion that shaped political culture so profoundly in the same period [1960s to 1970s]. Some of this suspicion came from within the disciplines it affected, but in every case it was at least reinforced by vulnerability to the suspicion of outsiders, often expressed in an explicitly political arena [p. 199].

The suspicion and skepticism account, in large part, for several developments. First, applied and university social research began to be clearly distinguished from one another in Denmark. Second, two specific and very different cultures were created in the area of social research. Third, there was a push toward quantification in the field of applied research. Bryant (1995, p. 127) indicated how important the balance between the two cultures is—and how damaging it would be if university research ceased to exist on campus: "If research moved off campus altogether into government and business in-house research units, or private commercial social research firms, there would be no such counterbalance—although the researchers so placed might find it easier to be of influence."

Social Research in Scandinavia

The situation was and still is very different in the other Scandinavian countries. Especially in Finland and Sweden, applied social research—including government-financed research—was performed in various organizational models of collaboration between university research and nonuniversity research units.

The central difference between applied social research in Denmark and the other Nordic countries is the organizational separation. Denmark chose to follow a line of a very clear separation between university and applied social research, whereas in the other Nordic countries, there are several types of cooperation and organization of applied and university social research.

Most important, in other Nordic countries, state-funded applied social research is much more integrated into the sociological institutes at the universities. Borrowing an observation that Alvin Gouldner made after visiting Sweden in 1969, Swedberg (1994, p. 194) characterized the Swedish situation as follows: "It seemed to me that Swedish sociology was of one piece with Swedish culture, most particularly with respect to the consensus that was given concerning the importance of using formalized, systematic and external methodologies. It was my impression that there is no group of sociologists anywhere in the world today who, more than those in Sweden, have a clearer and more agreed-upon view of the standards and values to which good sociology should conform." The combination of a strong political tradition for social engineering in the Swedish Social Democratic Party in the 1930s and the consensus on methodology that struck Gouldner gave Swedish sociology a much stronger tradition for participation in political and administrative research and evaluation.

In Denmark, the sharp division between applied social research and university sociology reflects the classic features of the two cultures that Snow ([1963] 1993) generally described as closedness and loss of scientific communication, acceptance, debate, and mutual criticism. In the golden years of Danish sociology, from 1960 to around 1980, both cultures bloomed, but the gap never closed. In the few turbulent years that followed 1968, the scene was dominated by very sharp conflicts between the rather narrow positivism at the Institute of Sociology and many new critical and Marxist sociological traditions. These new sociologies took up the heritage of classic continental European sociology and social philosophy, as well as theories of political change. In the late 1960s and early 1970s, the rediscovery of European sociology's classical roots combined with the student movement's radical concepts of social change also sharpened the focus on social scientists' obligation to use sociological knowledge to inform, reform, or act. These issues have always been central in the traditions of European sociology.

In postwar Danish sociology, however, this tradition for public political activism that combined social studies with social reforms was displaced by the dominant positivistic idea of neutral scientific knowledge (scientism) combined with social engineering. The 1970s saw the arrival of a new sociological discourse in Denmark with a number of new sociologies taking up the problems of how to use sociology and how to act as sociologists offering knowledge to society. The new sociologies covered a broad area, including cultural, hermeneutic and critical, Marxist, and feminist sociologies.

The same period, 1960 through 1980, was also a golden age for applied social research, especially the SFI. A number of new applied social research institutions were established. There was a great demand for large-scale social surveys to describe and analyze social problems in this period of Danish society's modernization. The SFI acquired many more researchers and grew even faster in its technical infrastructure. The majority of the studies performed in this period can be described as empirical and statistical surveys of social problem areas. The results were to be used in political decision making or to legitimize existing reforms.

Throughout the 1980s, the situation between the two cultures in Danish sociology slowly changed from conflicts "between empty theoreticism and blind empiricism" (Bourdieu, 1988, p. 777) or, in the words of C. Wright Mills (1961, p. 74), from "methodological inhibition" and "the fetishism of Concept" to different attempts to cooperate in practical research. This period witnessed a broader acceptance of other, more qualitative types of data and a growing integration of university social research in practical studies.

Danish Evaluation Traditions

In the history of applied social research in Denmark, it is easy to find aspects of evaluation in almost all empirical studies, as evaluation in a very broad sense is an integral part of the study of social life. Evaluation is involved in the selection of problems and research questions, as well as in the final results. As Lindblom (1990, p. 146) observed, "Given the character of evaluation, social scientists can hardly escape it." Yet it has been only within the past fifteen years that Danish social scientists have specifically designed and applied social research methods to answer evaluation questions asked not by social scientists themselves but by users of applied research.

A number of recent studies on Danish evaluation research summarize the major tendencies in different areas (Albæk, 1993, 1995; Albæk and Winter, 1993; Hansson, 1993, 1997; Rebien, 1996). Except for Rebien's study, which examined the Danish development aid evaluation, they all focus on evaluations performed in relation to the welfare state's development and the public sector's modernization (sometimes labeled "new public management"). In addition, they all focus on labor market and social policy reforms.

In spite of smaller differences, these studies agree on a general description of the situation. They locate central problems in the lack of a systematic use and discussion of evaluation theory and methodology, as well as in the lack of general social theory and methodology. A recent paper from one of the applied social research institutes, the Institute of Local Government Studies–Denmark (AKF), a local government research institution, points to the surprising deficit of professional networks and organization between evaluators in a small country such as Denmark, as well as to the absence of organized education in evaluation research (Rieper, 1996).

To present a picture of the many aspects of Danish evaluation research, it is helpful to supply a kind of typology or classification. In the evaluation literature, there are a number of descriptive typologies or classifications. Patton (1986) distinguished between the scientific, alternative, and utilization-focused paradigms. Guba and Lincoln (1989) proposed four evaluation generations: measurement, description, judgment, and responsive-constructivist. These studies' findings are examples of classifications based on criteria derived from evaluation research itself.

It is central to this chapter's argument, however, that evaluation research be understood as a part of applied social research. Today, it may be the largest and most important part. Therefore, one should look less for descriptive classifications and more for the ongoing discussions of applied social research, with its critical focus on the failures of the social engineering model in the 1970s (Albæk, 1988; Lindblom, 1959, 1990).

In a discussion of sociology's practicality and application, Bryant (1995) created four classifications of applied social research, according to different concepts and understandings of the production and use of knowledge in each category. The *social engineering model* is based on the idea of a technical, neutral intervention in social affairs, quite close to Snow's technical, natural science culture. The other three models are all based on different concepts of how to use social science knowledge and how to intervene in social affairs. They include the *enlightenment model,* the *interactive model,* and the *dialogical model.* These latter three models can be understood as subdivisions and specifications of what Snow described as a humanistic, interpretative science culture. In the remainder of this chapter, I will try to present a picture of Danish evaluation research, using these categories.

Social Engineering Model. The social engineering model, so named by Popper ([1945] 1995), is rooted in the tradition of positivistic sociology and is associated with quantitative techniques and large-scale empirical data collection: "The engineer or the technologist approaches institutions rationally as means to serve certain ends, and as a technologist he judges them wholly according to their appropriateness, efficiency, simplicity, etc." (p. 24). This model aims at identifying and describing problems and at presenting relevant information neutrally to whichever client needs to make policy changes. This model dominated Danish evaluation research from the start of organized evaluation research up through recent years. As described earlier, evaluation research was always embedded in the organizational and scientific frame of applied social research in Denmark's few large social research institutions. For more than ten years, the field of evaluation research more or less followed exactly the same development as applied sociology.

The pronounced criticism of this model in Danish and international social science that was formulated in the late 1960s (and that continues to the present) did not influence research procedures in evaluation research, because the majority of this debate took place outside the culture of applied social research. The discussion and criticism of positivism developed around the social sciences in the universities, not in the institutions in the field of practical evaluation research. Kalleberg (1995, pp. 11–12) noted that this is not only a Danish problem: "Also in the Norwegian and general European sociology, where the positivistic interpretation of sociology as a science has not been accepted during the last 2–3 decades, we still have a shadow theory of positivism, manifesting itself in the ordinary distortions of research designs."

Of the evaluations that were planned and conducted from a social engineering point of view and that used a clear but latent positivistic research approach, most were performed by the two large applied social research institutions, SFI and AKF, using their long traditions of large-scale, empirical surveys. These evaluations are characterized by the absence of the following elements: a discussion of the relevance and necessity of their survey procedures, a discussion of what kind of knowledge is thereby produced, a reference to a relevant social policy or sociological theories and knowledge, and a reference to the international evaluation discussion about methodology and theory in the field of program evaluation. An example of such evaluations is the evaluation of the large social policy and development program, Ministry for Social Affairs Development Programme (SUM), which took place from 1988 through 1992.

It is not only on this more general level that one can criticize the SUM evaluations for their naive positivistic concepts of reality. The SUM evaluators themselves had to conclude that it had "been difficult to document secure and reliable results" (Jensen, 1992) to the evaluation questions formulated by the program committee. Other researchers have criticized these evaluations for seriously omitting central problem areas that easily could have been included in discussions of actual social policy theory. Because of these omissions, it is not possible to evaluate and analyze a number of important questions in the large social policy experiment arena (Hansson, 1993). A great number of evaluations on a much smaller scale have followed the same general concept of evaluation as social engineering based on a positivistic research design (Albæk, 1993; Hansson, 1997). The situation is much the same for the Danish development aid evaluation in the 1980s (Rebien, 1996).

Judging from a number of "handbooks" and "toolboxes" on survey-based internal evaluations published by the Ministry of Finance (Finansministeriet, 1996), it is reasonable to argue that internal evaluations are becoming much more widespread in Denmark, especially as part of administrative control, information management, and organizational education. The Danish government has recently promoted the use of internal evaluations as instruments of modernization and quality control of institutions and organizations in the public sector. Evaluations of efficiency and user studies are particularly emphasized. Internal evaluation is largely compatible with a social engineering approach. This is evident not only from developments in Denmark but also from the literature on internal evaluation that points to influences from internal auditing procedures and methodologies and that identifies this practice as an instrument of organizational development.

Evaluations are about valuing policies and programs. Hence, the claimed value neutrality of social engineering results in either a forced omission of any discussion of value problems or in what Lindblom (1990) calls heroic attempts to escape from the problem of value; modes of escape include using technical instruments and quantifications, such as the cost-benefit analysis or Pareto optimality, to claim neutrality. The problem of values and the ethics of social and political interventions are left unsolved by the social engineering model's claim of neutrality for its evaluations.

Enlightenment and Interactive Models. Bryant presented the models of enlightenment and interaction as responses to the criticisms and problems that the social engineering model met. Both of Bryant's models emphasize the rational use of the knowledge produced by applied social science. The enlightenment model stresses the importance of presenting knowledge to the public, not just to an elite group. The interaction model stresses the interaction between applied research and policymakers and focuses more explicitly on the complexities in advocacy, policy, and decision making. I have chosen to treat the two models together, because there is still a limited amount of Danish evaluation research outside the social engineering model.

One of the most interesting evaluations of this type has been conducted in the field of research evaluation. The political interest in controlling and steering publicly financed research has never been stronger and has often resulted in very heated debates about productivity in university research, followed by discussions of evaluating research. This discussion has served as the background for some successful attempts to develop a more reflexive and theoretically based model for evaluating research. Christiansen and Foss Hansen (1993), Foss Hansen (1995), and Foss Hansen and Holst Jørgensen (1995) have succeeded in combining evaluations in this field with the use of organizational theory, and they have developed an evaluation model that was used in a case study of two Danish social science institutes. The results of this evaluation and a theory of research evaluation based on these studies have influenced the debate on research evaluations. These results have also shifted the focus away from individual results and productivity based on quantitative indicators. Now, the focus is more on the organizational setting and environment for research (universities, institutes, working groups, and networks) and on the need for reflection and dialogue in this field. The study is a good example of how an evaluation explicitly takes up public discussions in a specific field—in this case, the field of university policy. In this way, it exerts a strong influence on the agenda for policy formation.

Other examples of Danish evaluation research with explicit intentions to enlighten policymaking include a study of alternative medical treatment (Launsø, 1995) that evaluates the impact of how of people under treatment construct reality, rather than relying on the traditional medical diagnosis and professional expertise. In the area of evaluating adult education, a research group at Roskilde University has published a number of evaluation studies (Weber, 1993) using a broad variety of methodologies from cultural studies, ethnography, and qualitative methods to discuss the importance of gender, culture, and participation in evaluation studies. Finally, another example of a study in the labor market area is an evaluation of experiments with different family-oriented job arrangements; this evaluation uses focus group interviews to promote the participants' views and experiences (Holt and Thaulow, 1996). This is one of few evaluation studies by SFI to employ methodologies that differ from the traditional survey design, which is almost SFI's trademark. This may signify some movement away from the survey tradition and a slow withering away of the gap between the two cultures in evaluation.

Dialogical Model. According to Bryant (1995, p. 142), "The dialogical model of applied social research is similar to the interactive one except in its approach to methodology and its orientation to ordinary men and women and lay knowledge." The dialogical model is a broad model that couples the production of social scientific knowledge with the fundamental critique of the rational science knowledge—a critique that social scientists from Habermas to Giddens have put on the field's agenda. Dialogical models assume a hermeneutic understanding of reality in research. In the international evaluation research discussion, this has recently been formulated as an understanding of evaluations as a hermeneutic enterprise (Saxi, 1996; Schwandt, 1997). In Denmark, action research and other forms of interventional social research (or dialogical research, in Bryant's words) were taken up after 1968.

The criticism of established social science—whether it was the traditional logical positivism dominating the social sciences at the universities or the practical empiricist survey type of sociology practiced at the institutions for applied social research—implied a renewal of the problems of interests and knowledge in social science. This new criticism resulted in many different attempts to solve the problems of "praxis," or questions about the production and use of social scientific knowledge. In the end, the criticism led to what may be labeled a "fragmentation" of sociology—a fragmentation based on a critical sociology, deeply embedded in a society in which crisis and change are the normal situation, and opposed to a static and harmonic sociology that lacks social relevance (Bech and Bonns, 1984; Lemert, 1995). One outcome of this process was action research, which does not have the same long and outstanding tradition in the social sciences and evaluation research in Denmark as in Norway (Baklien, 1993).

Dialogical evaluations in most cases are undertaken by evaluators who are associated not with the large applied social research institutions but with smaller research groups in the universities. These evaluators use critical concepts of social theory and methodology, which have gradually been gaining influence in Danish sociology since the 1970s. A number of evaluation projects in this area have attempted to formulate and discuss central problems of action research theory in order to develop solutions to the classical action research conflict between the deep, often personal, involvement with the research object and values and the need to secure theoretical and methodological clarity and distance (Toulmin, 1996).

An outstanding example of action-based evaluation research in Denmark is the Consensus Conferences. This example demands special attention because, over a ten-year period, it has grown into a well-functioning model for a democratic technology assessment (Hansen, Danielsen, and Ravn, 1992; Mayer and Geurts, 1996; Street, 1997). Consensus Conferences were originally developed by a group of sociologists at the Danish Board of Technology Assessment, a state-funded group governed by representatives of political parties and interest groups that advises the Danish Parliament.

The normal procedure for a Consensus Conference is to set up a panel of ten to fifteen laypersons, who spend three days questioning an expert panel and discussing the experts' answers and statements with a broader audience. On the third day, the panel concludes the evaluation with a report and presents it to an audience and to the press. Consensus Conferences have addressed a large number of important, publicly debated issues of technology, including gene technology, irradiation, food technologies, traffic technologies, and information technologies. Consensus Conferences have often had a great impact on how political questions about new technologies have been formulated and put on the political agenda. In recent years, this model for involving laypersons in political debates and evaluations of new technologies has aroused a certain amount of interest in other European countries.

Another example of action research and evaluation in the area of work and technology is a project based on the use of future-creating workshops and the systematic use of work experience. The project called "Industry and Happiness" aims to use the interaction between the research group and a group of female workers in the fishing industry to produce new knowledge about how to make their work situation more fulfilling (Nielsen, 1996; Nielsen, Olsén, and Aagaard Nielsen, 1996).

Evaluations inspired by action research have taken place in areas such as education, work studies, occupational risk studies, health studies, implementation of new technologies, and organizational change and technology assessment. The formative evaluations of the Cultural Centre Development Project (Høgsbro, 1990) that a research group performed are typical for a growing number of evaluation projects, in which the dialogue between the local initiators and the researchers produces information to be used locally during the course of the project; the evaluation does not have a top-down perspective. In the social sector, Hegland (1997) has experimented with participation-based evaluations of local social policy development projects.

Danish Evaluation Research Today

Danish evaluation research shows a broad and differentiated picture with a dominance of traditional, survey-based evaluations. The preponderance of positivist interpretations and methodologies inside a broader operational concept of social engineering in Danish evaluation research is not surprising when one considers the dominance of applied social research institutions in evaluation research, as well as the two-culture problem described earlier. For two decades, the discussion of critical sociology in the wake of the student movement has been confined to the university environment, while applied social research has continued having a practical orientation.

Even today, most evaluations use predominantly empirical methods, and "the positivist quantitativists" (Bourdieu, 1991, p. 381) still dominate Danish evaluation research, as well as other areas of applied social science. Philosophical supporters of neopositivism are almost impossible to find today, but the methodologies associated with neopositivism and causal explanations based on a concept that value-free data can represent "reality" have not disappeared in evaluation research. Greene (1994) has named this kind of evaluation research "postpositivistic," to underline that these attitudes toward empirical research, still dominant in evaluation research, have a long history in sociology and philosophy. Porter (1995) emphasized that this kind of evaluation is closely linked to traditional ideas of efficiency and accountability, rules and standards, which places this type of evaluation rather close to auditing. Given the growth of internal evaluation, closely linked to organizational and managerial interests, there is reason to fear that the positivistic and empiricist approach to evaluation research will continue, along with a kind of secrecy while such evaluations are performed outside the critical scrutiny of professionals and the public.

The existence of a dominant, very technical, quantitative, and methodology-oriented evaluation culture in Denmark with close links to applied social research institutions supports this argument. Other evaluation cultures are less incorporated in large research organizations and have roots in different critical traditions in sociology, consultancy evaluations, and attempts to develop evaluations that focus on social change and user involvement, such as action research.

Yet, the prospects for enlightenment, interactive, and dialogical models of research have never been so promising as today. The use of alternative strategies and methodologies in evaluations is growing rapidly around the world and in Denmark, making room for participatory and action research–based evaluations. Can this "new wave" in evaluation research withstand the demands of bureaucracies and public decision makers to focus on accountability and quantification (Alvesson and Willmott, 1996; Porter, 1995)? Although there are examples of interactive evaluations from the large applied research institutions (Holt and Thaulow, 1996), SFI recently introduced the Central Social Research Register, which combines access to all public registry information with large databases that contain the results of numerous empirical surveys, and the official statistical databanks. This register can easily be used for quantitative and statistics-based evaluations of the outcomes of several public policy interventions and reforms.

Conclusion

The way Danish evaluation research has developed over the last ten to fifteen years is best understood in light of the two cultures that exist in Danish social science: an applied and a university-based social science. The divergence of these cultures is illustrated most clearly by the way in which sociology has developed.

The original close relation between applied social research, government, and administration—as well as the corresponding isolation of university social research from large-scale empirical studies—caused the two social science cultures to develop. In the 1980s, evaluation research grew naturally out of the applied social research culture, which emphasized empiricist methodology, quantification, and fact-finding social surveys. In the same period, Denmark began to modernize, as did most Western countries. Social reflexivity based on sociological concepts was no longer limited to the scientific community but became part of society (Beck, 1997; Lemert, 1995). Social understanding incorporated social theory in all areas of society and became part of the normal reflections and understanding of everyday life. In Bude's ironic words (1994), everybody has become a barefoot sociologist.

In this process of modernizing society and state, a need has evolved for a more flexible and open kind of evaluation research. This contrasts sharply with the method social scientists have embraced for years, a "highly specialized empirical social research [that] presumes a constancy of categories and hence a high and actually rather rare social stability" (Beck, 1997, p. 18). Over time, the stiff division into two cultures in Danish evaluation research and sociology has been undermined by the social need for new forms of evaluation research. It was originally possible for new types to develop because in the other culture—the universities—new critical sociologies with innovative methodologies and experience in involving people in research had been developing for a number of years. The coming years will reveal whether the tendencies of new critical approaches to Danish evaluation research can flourish.

References

Agersnap, T. "Sociologi I Danmark før 1950" [Sociology in Denmark before 1950]. In F. Hansson and K. A. Nielsen (eds.), *Dansk sociologis historie—et politiseret fag gennem brud og kontinuitet* [The history of Danish sociology—Through policy, conflicts, and continuity]. Copenhagen: Forlaget Sociologi, 1996.

Albæk, E. *Fra sandhed til information* [From truth to information]. Copenhagen: Akademisk forlag, 1988.

Albæk, E. "Evalueringsforskning I Norden" [Evaluation research in Scandinavia]. *Politica,* 1993, *25* (1), 6–26.

Albæk, E. "Between Knowledge and Power: Utilization of Social Science in Public Policy Making." *Policy Science,* 1995, *28,* 79–100.

Albæk, E. "Why All This Evaluation? Theoretical Notes and Empirical Observations on the Function and Growth of Evaluation, with Denmark as an Illustrative Case." *Canadian Journal of Program Evaluation,* 1996, *11* (2), 1–34.

Albæk, E., and Winter, S. "Evaluering I Danmark—Rationalitet eller politisk våben?" [Evaluation research in Denmark—Rationality or political weapon?] *Politica,* 1993, *25* (1), 27–46.

Alvesson, M., and Willmott, H. *Making Sense of Management: A Critical Introduction.* Thousand Oaks, Calif.: Sage, 1996.

Andersen, H., Blegvad, B., and Blegvad, M. "Contemporary Sociology in Denmark." In R. P. Mohan and A. S. Wilke (eds.), *International Handbook of Contemporary Developments in Sociology.* London: Mansell, 1994.

Andersson, B., and Dabrowski, A. "Sociolgiens akademiske, administrative og kommercielle felter, 1950–1970" [The academic, administrative, and commercial fields of sociology, 1950–1970]. In F. Hansson and K. A. Nielsen (eds.), *Dansk sociologis historie—et politiseret fag gennem brud og kontinuitet* [The history of Danish sociology—Through policy, conflicts, and continuity]. Copenhagen: Forlaget Sociologi, 1996.

Baklien, B. "Evalueringsforskning I Norge" [Evaluation research in Norway]. *Tidsskrift for samfunnsforskning,* 1993, *34* (3), 261–274.

Bech, U., and Bonns, W. "Soziologie und Modernisierung. Zur Ortsbestimmung der Verwendungsforschung" [Sociology and modernization. New contexts for applied social research]. *Soziale Welt,* 1984, *35,* 381–406.

Beck, U. *The Reinvention of Politics: Rethinking Modernity in the Global Social Order.* Cambridge, England: Polity Press, 1997.

Bierstedt, R. *American Sociological Theory: A Critical History.* Orlando, Fla.: Academic Press, 1981.

Boje, T. P., and Hort, S.E.O. "Scandinavia Between Utopia and Anarchy." In T. P. Boje and S.E.O. Hort (eds.), *Scandinavia in a New Europe.* Oslo: Scandinavia University Press, 1993.

Bourdieu, P. "Vive la Crise! For Heterodoxy in Social Science." *Theory and Society,* 1988, *17* (5), 773–788.

Bourdieu, P. "On the Possibility of a Field of World Sociology." In P. Bourdieu and J. S. Coleman (eds.), *Social Theory for a Changing Society.* Boulder, Colo.: Westview Press, 1991.

Bryant, C.G.A. *Practical Sociology: Post-Empiricism and the Reconstruction of Theory and Application.* Cambridge, England: Polity Press, 1995.

Bude, H. "1968 und die Soziologie" [1968 and sociology]. *Soziale Welt,* 1994, *45* (2), 242–254.

Christiansen, J. K., and Foss Hansen, H. *Forskningsevaluering I teori og praksis. Organisering, netværk og publicering* [Research evaluation in theory and practice. Organizations, networks, and publishing]. Copenhagen: Samfundslitteratur, 1993.

Finansministeriet (ed.). *Evaluering og effektsikring. Vejledning* [Evaluation and securing efficiency. A guide]. Copenhagen: Ministry of Finance, 1996.

Foss Hansen, H. "Organizing for Quality: A Discussion of Different Evaluation Methods as Means for Improving Quality in Research." *Science Studies,* 1995, *8* (1), 36–52.

Foss Hansen, H., and Holst Jørgensen, B. *Styring af forskning. Kan forskningsindikatorer anvendes?* [Managing research. Are indicators useful?] Copenhagen: Samfundslitteratur, 1995.

Greene, J. C. "Qualitative Program Evaluation: Practice and Promise." In N. Denzin and Y. Lincoln (eds.), *Handbook of Qualitative Research.* Thousand Oaks, Calif.: Sage, 1994.

Guba, E. G., and Lincoln, Y. S. *Fourth Generation Evaluation.* Thousand Oaks, Calif.: Sage, 1989.

Hansen, T., Danielsen, O., and Ravn, J. *Technology Assessment in Denmark: A Briefing.* Copenhagen: The Danish Board of Technology, 1992.

Hansson, F. "Evalueringsforskning og sociologisk teori" [Evaluation research and sociological theory]. *Dansk sociologi,* 1993, *4* (4), 20–38.

Hansson, F. "Evaluation Traditions in Denmark: Critical Comments and Perspectives." *Evaluation,* 1997, *3* (1), 85–96.

Hansson, F., and Nielsen, K. A. (eds.). *Dansk sociologis historie—et politiseret fag gennem brud og kontinuitet* [The history of Danish sociology—Through policy, conflicts, and continuity]. Copenhagen: Forlaget Sociologi, 1996.

Hegland, T. J. *From a Thousand Flowers to Targeted Development.* Copenhagen: Copenhagen Business School, 1997.

Høgsbro, K. *Kulturcenterundersøgelsen 2* [Report Two on the culture centers]. Copenhagen: Udviklingscenter for Folkeoplysning og Voksenundervisning, 1990.

Holt, H., and Thaulow, I. *Erfaringer fra et udviklingsprojekt om familievenlige arbejdspladser* [Experience from a project on development of family-friendly arrangements on the job]. Copenhagen: Socialforskningsinstituttet, 1996.

Jensen, M. K. *Slut-SUM. En sammenfatning af projekterfaringerne fra Socialministeriets Udviklingsprogram* [The end of SUM. The final report on the experience from the projects in the Social Ministry of Development Program]. Copenhagen: Socialforskningsinstituttet, 1992.

Kalleberg, R. *Action Research as Science and Profession in the Discipline of Sociology.* Oslo: Department of Sociology, University of Oslo, 1995.

Launsø, L. *Det alternative behandlingsområde. Brug og udvikling, rationalitet og paradigmer* [The alternative health treatment. Uses and development, rationality and paradigms]. Copenhagen: Akademisk Forlag, 1995.

Lemert, C. *Sociology After the Crisis.* Boulder, Colo.: Westview Press, 1995.

Lindblom, C. E. "The Science of 'Muddling Through.'" *Public Administration Review,* 1959, *19,* 79–88.

Lindblom, C. E. *Inquiry and Change: The Troubled Attempt to Understand and Shape Society.* New Haven, Conn.: Yale University Press, 1990.

Mayer, I. S., and Geurts, J. L. "Consensus Conferences as Participatory Policy Analysis: A Methodological Contribution to the Social Management of Technology." In *Technical Expertise and Public Decisions.* Proceedings of the IEEE 1996 International Symposium on Technology and Society. Princeton, N.J.: Princeton University, 1996.

Mills, C. W. *The Sociological Imagination.* New York: Grove Atlantic, 1961.

Nielsen, B. S., Olsén, P., and Aagaard Nielsen, K. "From Silent to Talkative Participants: A Discussion of Technique as Social Construction." *Economic and Industrial Democracy,* 1996, *3,* 359–386.

Nielsen, K. A. *Arbejdets sociale orientering. En industrisociologisk undersøgelse af forholdet imellem arbejdslivsdemokrati og mulighederne for bæredygtighed I industrielle moderniseringsprocesser* [The social orientation of work. An industrial sociological investigation of the relation between workers' participation and the possibilities of sustainable industrial production]. Copenhagen: Forlaget Sociologi, 1996.

Patton, M. Q. *Utilization-Focused Evaluation.* (2nd ed.) Thousand Oaks, Calif.: Sage, 1986.

Popper, K. *The Open Society and Its Enemies.* New York: Routledge, 1995. (Originally published 1945.)

Porter, T. M. *Trust in Numbers: The Pursuit of Objectivity in Science and Public Life.* Princeton, N.J.: Princeton University Press, 1995.

Rebien, C. C. *How to Evaluate Development Aid: A Theory and Methodology in the Making.* Copenhagen: Samfundslitteratur, 1996.

Rieper, O. *Bør Danmark have en evalueringspolitik?* [Does Denmark need an evaluation policy?] Copenhagen: Institute of Local Government Studies–Denmark (AKF), 1996.

Saxi, H. P. *Evaluering som hermeneutikk* [Evaluation as hermeneutics]. Bergen, Norway: LosSenteret Notat., 1996.

Schwandt, T. A. "Evaluation as Practical Hermeneutics." *Evaluation,* 1997, *3* (1), 69–83.

Snow, C. P. *The Two Cultures.* Cambridge, England: Cambridge University Press, 1993. (Originally published 1963.)

Sørensen, T. *Social-statistiske undersøgelser over byarbejderes og landarbejderes levevilkår, arbejdsulykker, børnedødelighed og økonomisk og erhvervsbetinget dødelighed I anden halvdel af det 19. århundrede. Vol. 1 & 2.* [Social-statistical investigations into the conditions of life for town and country workers, work accidents, child mortality, and economic and work-related mortality in the second half of the nineteenth century. Volumes One and Two]. Copenhagen: Selskabet for Udgivelse af Kilder til Dansk Historie, 1984. (Originally published 1880.)

Street, P. "Scenario Workshops: A Participatory Approach to Sustainable Living?" *Futures,* 1997, *29* (2), 139–158.

Swedberg, R. "Contemporary Sociology in Sweden." In R. P. Mohan and A. S. Wilke (eds.), *International Handbook of Contemporary Developments in Sociology.* London: Mansell, 1994.

Thomas, A. H. "Social Democracy in Denmark." In W. E. Paterson and A. E. Thomas (eds.), *Social Democratic Parties in Western Europe*. London: Croom Helm, 1977.

Toulmin, S. "Concluding Methodological Reflections: Elitism and Democracy Among Sciences." In S. Toulmin and B. Gustavsen (eds.), *Beyond Theory: Changing Organizations Through Participation*. Amsterdam: Benjamins, 1996.

Weber, K. (ed.). *Evalueringsforskning mellem politik og videnskab. Artikler fra Workshop vedr. metodeproblemer I evalueringsforskning under Netværket vedr. udvikling af voksenpædagogik som teoriområde* [Evaluation research between policy and science. Contributions from a workshop on methodology in evaluation research organized by the network on adult education]. Roskilde, Denmark: Roskilde University Center, 1993.

FINN HANSSON is a sociologist at the Copenhagen Business School Library working with evaluation theory and the sociology of science.

The author provides a brief history of the role that evaluation has played in Norwegian industrial development efforts and offers a critical commentary on the current state of the art.

Evaluation of Industrial Development in Norway

Hans Torvatn

This chapter discusses the purpose, role, methodology, and use of evaluations in contemporary industrial development in Norway. There is a strong Norwegian tradition of evaluating industrial development, but as is the case with this evaluation activity internationally, there is relatively little theory development in Norway (Shapira and Roesner, 1996).

Development of Work Life and Industry in Norway

Three models have guided the development of Norwegian industry since World War II (Elvemo, Fossen, and Levin, 1991). In the two decades immediately after the war, a central planning model facilitated national reconstruction. That was followed by a cooperation-consensus model that emphasized the democratization of work life. Currently, we are in the midst of an industrial modernization model in which the overall goal is industrial restructuring and innovating in order to maintain and improve international competitiveness. Table 5.1 gives an overview of the models.

Central Planning. After World War II, the Labor Party came to power and was unchallenged for twenty years. Social economists in the Department of Finance tried to reconstruct Norwegian industry through planned, budgeted, subsidized, and controlled industrial development. Large government- owned and -operated factories were built, a price-control system was established, agricultural production was protected, and certain commodities were subsidized. During this period of rapid economic expansion and growth, fueled in part by Marshall aid, few if any of the various measures initiated by the Department of Finance were evaluated. The reconstruction of industry, as well as the parallel construction of

**Table 5.1. Developmental Models of Norwegian Industry
Since World War II**

	Central Planning	*Cooperation-Consensus*	*Industrial Modernization*
Period	1945–1965	1965–1981	1981–present
Goal	Rebuilding national industry after WWII	Improving working conditions, effectiveness, and democracy	Restructuring and revitalizing Norwegian industry
Major features	Receiving Marsall aid	Encouraging a high degree of involvement	Removal of protection
	Instituting price-control system	Using consensus as basis for change	Identification of (new) technology as key to success
	Subsidizing certain commodities	Developing a participatory structure	Stronger emphasis on research
	Protecting agriculture and certain parts of industry	Experimenting in the industry	Scores of national plans and programs
	Constructing large government-owned and -operated factories		
Major actors	Department of Finance	Trade Union Council	Innovation system
		Confederation of Employers	
		Department of Work and Interior	
		STS researchers	
Results	Successfully rebuilding industry	Creating laws on work environment, safety, absenteeism, and wages	Restructuring industry
	Increasing standard of living	Permitting worker participation in boards	Improving innovation capacity
		Establishing various agreements between trade unions and employers	Developing the economy Creating an open economy
Evaluation	Very little evaluating	Evaluating industrial experiments, providing input for laws and agreements	Increased evaluating of individual plans, programs, and agencies

the welfare state, was shaped by political ideological agreements between the labor unions and the Social Democratic Party. This reconstruction, like the construction of the welfare state, was planned but never evaluated.

Cooperation-Consensus. The Norwegian reconstruction effort was successful. Norway managed to build an industrial base and boost its national productivity and gross national product. As the reconstruction period ended in the early 1960s, the stage was set for reforms in work life. Through the Norwegian Industrial Democracy Project, the cooperation-consensus model became the most prominent framework for work life development.

The two cornerstones of this model were a high degree of involvement of major stakeholders in industrial development and consensus among them. The workplace was only developed after management and labor achieved consensus. The aim of this process was to democratize the workplace and, through this, to democratize the whole society. Significantly, this process was also seen as a method of improving productivity. Efficiency and democracy were considered to go hand in hand.

Starting in the 1960s, the "big three" in Norwegian work life—the Trade Union Council, the Confederation of Employers, and the Ministry of Work and Interior—supported a comprehensive set of reforms that became known as the Norwegian Industrial Democracy Project.

The project began when the left wing of the trade union demanded more worker control of the workplace. The Trade Union Council and the Confederation of Employers decided to research the matter. The Institute of Social Research in Industry (IFIM), in collaboration with the Tavistock Institute in London, conducted an inquiry into the role of the workers' directors (managers). It was found that whether or not workers' directors were outstanding performers, their presence had no effect on the feelings of alienation on the shop floor. To reduce alienation and improve productivity, it was proposed that workers should directly participate in decisions about what was done at their own level. This idea was widely discussed in the two confederations and in the press. A consensus was reached that direct participation should be tried (Trist, 1981).

A set of experiments in selected companies were carried out, using sociotechnical-systems (STS) models to improve efficiency at the shop floor level. Work life researchers played a key role in these experiments, designing as well as evaluating them. The researchers were quite involved in the project. In its earliest phase (the sleeping bag phase), they literally lived in companies and controlled the whole process. In the project's second phase (the toolmaker phase), the researchers developed a set of tools they could employ in several companies, and over a longer period of time. Based on their analysis of the company (employing their tools), the researchers offered fairly detailed suggestions for organizational development of the participating companies. Finally, in the third phase (the do-it-yourself phase), the researchers taught workers and management STS principles and ways to use the tools. The companies could now develop themselves without researcher interference (Elden, 1979).

The projects had had fairly specific goals in terms of increasing productivity and, less specifically, in terms of democratizing the workplace. The researchers found that the experiments demonstrated the value (increased productivity) of having workers help design and implement change processes. When the results were reported, it was assumed that these good results would inspire the whole industry to take up STS thinking. For a variety of reasons, however, STS thinking did not enjoy wide acceptance in all sectors of Norwegian industry.

Hence, the alliance of industry, labor, and government focused on institutionalizing the cooperation-consensus model by establishing it in various laws and agreements. In the mid-1970s, laws about workers' rights to board representation, regulation of work environment, health and safety, and absenteeism were passed. In addition, trade unions and the Confederation of Employers made several agreements specifying how organizational developmental processes should be carried out.

None of the laws and agreements made in this period have been evaluated per se. Evaluation was limited to evaluation of the actual experiments on STS models in pilot companies. It is therefore difficult to assess the impact of these laws and agreements. The industrial democracy project did leave an evaluational heritage, however, by establishing a tradition for action research and by enabling research agencies to carry out evaluations. The project created a network of researchers who were oriented toward action research and work life studies, who focused on industrial development, and who helped establish contract research agencies that worked with industrial development topics. Thus, when the next phase of industrial development began, Norway had a set of researchers interested in action research and industrial development, as well as a set of institutions to carry out contract research work such as evaluations.

Industrial Modernization. In the 1980s, Norway experienced an economic recession. Even though income from North Sea oil lessened the recession's impact, other Norwegian industries performed poorly, especially the large, government-owned factories. External pressure to open more of Norwegian markets to foreign competition was increasing, but it was obvious that Norwegian industry could not compete internationally. Two major needs were identified. The first was to restructure parts of Norwegian industry; the second was to enhance industrial competitiveness and innovative capability.

To accomplish these goals, the government needed agencies that could analyze industrial structure; identify development needs; and plan, initiate, fund, implement, and evaluate a variety of efforts to enhance competitiveness. The government also sought assistance in identifying and creating industrial opportunities and in developing mechanisms for promoting and implementing new technology and training. It was also necessary to coordinate these efforts and to inform the potential beneficiaries about their possibilities. All this became the responsibility of a variety of agencies collectively constituting the "innovation system." Some of these agencies existed before 1980, but their tasks and relationships were redefined to improve their performance. Other agencies arose in the 1980s to fill specific functions.

The most important agencies in this "system" are the Ministry of Work and Interior, the Department of Industry, the Norwegian Science Council, the Regional Development Fund, the Confederation of Employers, and the Trade

Union Council. These agencies plan, coordinate, fund, and initiate various efforts for industrial modernization. (The Trade Union Council and the Confederation of Employers fund relatively few projects, but they play central roles in planning and initiating projects, and their support is important for an effort's success.)

Implementation of the efforts is usually left to other, more "operational" agencies. These agencies must promote the various efforts, recruit participants, and deliver the actual services. The services delivered can take a variety of forms, ranging from training programs, business assessments, information provision, and consulting services to implementation of technology, adaptation of research, and the performance of pure and applied research. Typical examples of operational agencies are contract research agencies, consulting firms, and project organizations set up specifically to implement a particular effort.

The industrial consulting and research agencies, as well as a number of independent consultants, have two major functions in the innovation system. The first is to develop new scientific knowledge and technology, including the necessary promotion, dissemination, transfer, and adaptation in industry. *Technology* here includes not simply hardware and software but also management techniques and principles. The second function is to disseminate knowledge of the industry's problems and needs, as well as the system's function and efficiency. In other words, the second function is evaluation.

The Evaluation System Within the Innovation System

The development of an innovation system for industrial revitalization was part of the general interest in reforming the welfare state. The interest in reforms in the 1980s was so great that it led one Norwegian policy analyst to call Norway an "experimenting society" (Olsen, 1993). Of course, all these innovations and experiments had to be summarized and analyzed, and the bureaucracy lacked the capacity, knowledge, and legitimacy to do this. Outsourcing to external evaluators thus became a common practice. The volume of evaluations in the 1980s rose along with the innovation system, thereby creating an evaluation system within the innovation system.

Contract research agencies are now the main actors in the field of industrial modernization evaluation. There is only one such actor from the university or college system—the Norwegian University of Science and Technology, which operates in tandem with IFIM. In addition to these agencies, private consultants conduct some evaluations. It is difficult, however, to determine the number and scope of evaluations that private consultants conduct, because these evaluations are not registered anywhere. Evaluators often have little formal training as evaluators. There are no degree programs in evaluation at the university or college level. The majority of evaluators specialize in the disciplines and fields of psychology, sociology, anthropology, education, and engineering. The evaluations that these actors perform are the focus of the rest of this chapter.

The Purpose and Use of Industrial Modernization Evaluations

All evaluations have three closely intertwined purposes: to support program management in program development, to report program outcomes, and to provide feedback from the participants in the program. Evaluations focus on such questions as the following: Was the program delivered to the target group as scheduled? Were the users satisfied with the program? What effects of the program can be identified? Of course, there are many variations on these questions, and evaluations also often address more local or site-specific concerns.

Program management uses evaluations as a tool to improve organizational efficiency by examining processes and problems in program implementation (Torvatn, 1993). In order to improve organizational efficiency, the evaluator has to investigate program implementation and program impact, the latter being the measure of success for the program.

The overall goal for all the industrial modernization efforts is the same— to increase the industry's global competitiveness. Of course, this is a long-term goal, and it could be effected in many ways. Direct evaluation of this long-term goal is rarely undertaken. Rather, the evaluator will identify a set of intermediate outcomes of the program that could be seen as a step toward long-term goals (Arbo, 1993).

User satisfaction is the most popular outcome measure employed, but not the only one. Other measures are used, depending on the activity in question. For example, in a program supporting development of strategic plans, the existence of such plans would be an outcome. In a program subsidizing small and medium-sized enterprises (SMEs) in hiring export managers, the continuation of the export manager position after subsidization could be used as a measure. If the effort were a funding scheme for development of a new product, the evaluator could investigate product development rates, eventual amount of sales from the new product, and so on.

The source of outcome information will almost always be participant feedback. Indeed, participant feedback is the major source of the evaluation's legitimacy. The evaluator has to collect information from participants, analyze it, and report it to program management and program funders. With no or little feedback from the participants, the evaluation will not be trusted (Torvatn, 1993).

These purposes (improving programs, reporting outcomes, and collecting participant feedback) shape evaluation methodology. Evaluation must be conducted in a way that provides quick answers to important questions, focuses on participants' experiences, and measures outcome.

Evaluation Methodology

The most prominent types of Norwegian evaluation methodology can be roughly classified with the following four categories: action research, implementation analysis, causal analysis, and ideal-reality analysis (Arbo, 1993; Bak-lien, 1993; Torvatn and Rønningsbakk, 1991).

Action Research. Action research is a strategy for using scientific methods to solve practical problems in a way that contributes to general social science theory and knowledge (Elden and Levin, 1991). Action research has a broad tradition in Norway, Sweden, and elsewhere, and it is far beyond the scope of this chapter to describe action research in general. Instead, I will focus on the particular version employed in Norwegian industrial modernization evaluation.

Within this tradition, the action research orientation describes a form of evaluation with close and continual cooperation between practitioners and eval-uators. This mode of cooperation was established in the 1960s and 1970s, before evaluation became popular and before evaluation theory arrived in Norway. In those earliest days of evaluation in Norway, evaluation theory was rarely employed at all, and the evaluator relied on an arsenal of social science methods.

As evaluation became more popular in the 1980s, the need for theory arose, and Norwegian evaluators turned to sources in the United States. When naturalistic and utilization-focused theories (Guba and Lincoln, 1981; Guba and Lincoln, 1989; Patton, 1986) arrived in Norway at the end of the 1980s, they were quickly employed by action researchers conducting evaluations.

Given the strong tradition of action research and evaluation in Norway, one might expect Norwegian evaluators to develop their own theories and models for action research–based evaluations, but only one model—"trailing research"—has been published so far. *Trailing research* is a blend of formative and summative evaluation approaches that relies on participants' high involve-ment in designing, implementing, and interpreting the knowledge constructed during the evaluation. Researchers seek to establish arenas for dialogue in which the various stakeholders (including the evaluators) can cogenerate new knowledge that is valid as a basis for action for all involved (Elden and Levin, 1991; Finne, Levin, and Nilssen, 1995).

Implementation Analysis. Implementation analysis deals with how an effort was carried out and with what furthered or hindered the desired effects. It is probably the most common type of evaluation of industrial moderniza-tion efforts.

The most common elements of such an analysis are progress (when the program was started, how much money has been spent, what the administra-tive routines are, and so on); recruitment of participants (procedures, prob-lems, results); a description of the participants (size, industrial sector, geographical location); and completion rates (how many participants com-pleted the whole program). In addition, there is often some measure of imple-mentation unique to the specific program. The level of attention given to these analyses varies considerably, from a one-page summary of program progress to a detailed analysis of every element.

Implementation analysis is closely linked to impact analysis. Several eval-uations employ some sort of program theory or model as part of this analysis. There seems to be a growing consensus on the need for a model to describe how the program is supposed to work, but there has been no agreement about what such models should include. There are examples of general purpose models, specific (sometimes causal) models developed for a particular evaluation, and procedures and guidelines for developing a program theory. I will discuss the last in detail.

A *program theory,* as understood by Finne, Levin, and Nilssen (1995), describes the program's logic and context and enables the evaluator to check on program progress and impact before the program is conducted. A key element in a program theory is the chain of reasoning. A *chain of reasoning* is an evaluation tool that was developed at IFIM. Finne and colleagues define it as "a combination of text and a graphic image which presents the activities of a program or project, the goals to be attained, additional assumptions and the links between them. Each actor may have a different chain of reasoning, or program theory, or cognitive map, which integrates their thoughts of the program" (p. 23). A full program theory also encompasses other elements not included in a chain of reasoning, such as a description of program context, the rationale underlying the program, experiences from similar earlier programs, and propositions about the program, if any. The theory is dynamic, and as time passes, it includes unintended impacts.

The chain of reasoning evaluation tool was used, for example, in the experimental program called "Managing the Integration of New Technology" (MINT), which the European Commission launched. The program aimed to improve SMEs' ability to adopt new technology. Seventeen European countries (including Norway) participated in the program. MINT's trademark activity was the use of consultants to develop an action plan for employing new technology in firms, in such a way as to fit in a firm's overall strategy.

Because this idea originated in a Norwegian program called "Business Development Using New Technology" (BUNT), it was decided that the Norwegian MINT (MINT-N) should test the effect of a revised version of the old BUNT participants' strategic plans. Thus, MINT-N was offered only to former BUNT participants.

Figure 5.1 shows the chain of reasoning for MINT-N. Arrows denote links between elements, as well as time flow. Solid arrows indicate links within the program; dashed arrows indicate weaker links with long time lags. Solid boxes are MINT-N activities; dashed boxes are prerequisites. The circle indicates a goal, as well as MINT-N's implicit vision.

The chain of reasoning describes the logic of MINT-N. A set of consultants (picked by the program) have the responsibility of approaching suitable SMEs (former BUNT participants) and offering MINT. If the company accepts participation, the consultant carries out a strategic analysis, using the strategy developed in BUNT as input and identifying economically sound innovation projects. The company and the consultant jointly prioritize these projects, revise the strategy, and develop a new action plan. The consultant leaves, and the company implements the measures in the action plan. If the program has functioned as planned, the company will have learned how to revise strategic

Figure 5.1. Original Chain of Reasoning for MINT-N, Derived from the Proposal

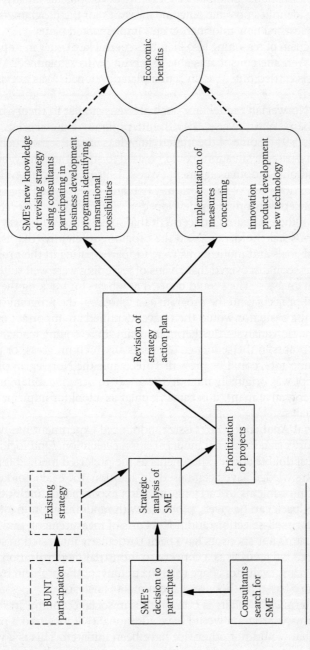

Source: Finne and Torvatn, 1996.

plans, use consultants, participate in business development programs, and identify transnational possibilities for future development. Finally, the chain of reasoning identifies possible outcome measures for the program—in this case, the SMEs learned new information and implemented plans.

The chain of reasoning also identifies several key issues in implementation analysis. Were the consultants able to recruit SMEs as planned? Was a strategic analysis carried out? Was an action plan developed? Was a revised strategy developed?

The Norwegian model described above is similar to theory-based evaluation (Chen, 1990; Weiss, 1996) and program logic models (Rush and Ogborne, 1991). Some of the underlying ideas are the same, such as the idea that theory-based evaluations could be used to strengthen the validity of evaluation without random assignment (Weiss, 1996). Norwegian evaluators were not aware, however, of the work of Chen and others when the chain of reasoning concept was originally developed in 1992 as part of an evaluation project. One of the evaluators' concerns at that time was to find a way to describe how various stakeholders viewed the program differently (that is, what their individual goals and motivations were for participating in the program).

It was soon discovered that chains of reasoning were well suited to implementation analysis. They could be used as a basis for tracking the progress of individual projects (and the program as a whole). If the program strayed from its track, the evaluator would then have identified an important event for the implementation analysis. Furthermore, chains of reasoning made it possible to establish points in the sequence of events at which progress, or preliminary impact indicators, could be probed. Thus, while the Norwegian program theory concept was originally intended as a way to describe different theories of action (a cognitive map), it became popular as a tool for implementation and impact analysis.

Causal Analysis. The classic randomized experiment has never been a part of Norwegian industrial modernization evaluation. Ontological and epistemological doubts about experiments as the preferred method for constructing new knowledge have been raised. In addition, the evaluator faces all sorts of practical problems in carrying out such experiments, including time lag before feedback can be given, problems with randomization in efforts relying on voluntary self-selection, additional costs of measurement, and so on. Neither evaluators nor sponsors have been particularly interested in such evaluations. Yet causal analysis is a concern in industrial modernization evaluation. In recent years, evaluators have tried to circumvent the problem by using program theory-based methods and additionality analysis.

The term *additionality* is borrowed from social economy. In strictest economic terms, a program would have additionality if it caused a project to be realized that would not otherwise have been initiated. This is a very limited concept, for a program could influence projects significantly in ways other than initiating it. For example, a program could influence the schedule, project quality, scale, and risk reduction. Finne and Torvatn (1996, p. 37) provide a more comprehensive definition: "Additionality is the difference between the benefits with which the program is associated and those that the company would have incurred with the most probable alternative use of its own resources." Regardless of which definition one uses, additionality is a counterfactual analysis. The fact is that program participation has occurred. Assessing what would have happened without this participation is thus counterfactual. We can never know for sure what would have happened without it, but we can still analyze what the counterfactual situation might have been.

In practice, the evaluator relies on a set of "What would you have done without the program?" questions for the participants. They are asked to state their interest in the service at full price, the new plans developed through the process, the likelihood that a particular project would have been carried out without the program, the scale at which it would have been undertaken, and so on. Based on the answers, the evaluator analyzes the program's additionality. The evaluation of MINT-N will serve as an example in Figure 5.2 and Table 5.2.

Figure 5.2 shows the firms' answer to the question "Without support from MINT, would the firm have done a similar project?" Approximately 40 percent of the companies would not have done such a project; for them, there is a definite release effect. Approximately another 40 percent, however, would have done a similar project, so they have no release effect.

Table 5.2 shows the answers to this question: "Looking at the most concrete measure in your MINT project, how well developed or concrete were the plans for that measure before the project started?" Of the firms, 6 percent found completely new measures, whereas another 6 percent managed to accomplish what they had failed to do before. The large majority of the firms

Figure 5.2. Release Effect of MINT-N

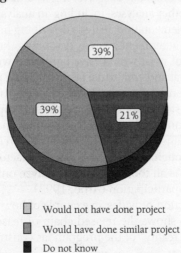

- Would not have done project
- Would have done similar project
- Do not know

Source: Finne and Torvatn, 1996.

Table 5.2. Concreteness of Plans Before Start-Up of MINT-N

How Concrete Were Your Previous Plans? (N=36)	Percentage of Companies
Had loose idea	47
Had commenced planning	41
Had unknown measure	6
Had aborted plan	6
Had little that was new	0

Source: Finne and Torvatn, 1996.

had some previous ideas, and almost half of these had begun making plans. Closer investigation revealed that these measures had been planned during the previous BUNT program, some three years ago, but had not been implemented before. Thus, MINT-N had limited ability to identify new measures, but was helpful in reviving old projects.

The examples from MINT-N are typical of an additionality analysis in Norwegian industrial modernization evaluation today. The analysis will usually employ more questions than the examples above, but the basic idea remains the same. The evaluators rely on participant feedback, and the approach is simple and direct.

It seems that few programs are able to alter the development of a firm radically. In some cases, it was found that the programs basically subsidized existing plans. In other cases, programs have had an important quality control function for development plans, and in others, timing has been the most important value enhanced.

Ideal-Reality Analysis. Ideal-reality analysis, a Norwegian evaluation tradition used in several fields of evaluation (Baklien, 1993), compares program ideals with the "reality" that the evaluator observes. It is a valuing process that involves the synthesis of several other analyses, including an analysis of program visions, goals, and plans; an implementation analysis describing how plans were carried out; an outcome or goal attainment analysis describing the observed "reality"; a counterfactual analysis of what would have happened without the effort; and some analysis of structural and contextual factors shaping program outcomes.

Given the broad consensus among stakeholders (including evaluators) about the underlying vision of increased industrial competitiveness, it is rare that evaluations of this kind analyze underlying values and visions. The appropriateness of specific plans and measures initiated to reach those visions are frequently evaluated, though. Analysis of contextual factors shaping outcomes is unfortunately rare. It is all too common to analyze only what happened to companies during their participation (Arbo, 1993).

The MINT-N evaluation provides an example of how different analyses are synthesized. Figure 5.3 shows the revised chain of reasoning for MINT and describes the observed "reality" of the program, as constructed by the evaluators during the evaluation.

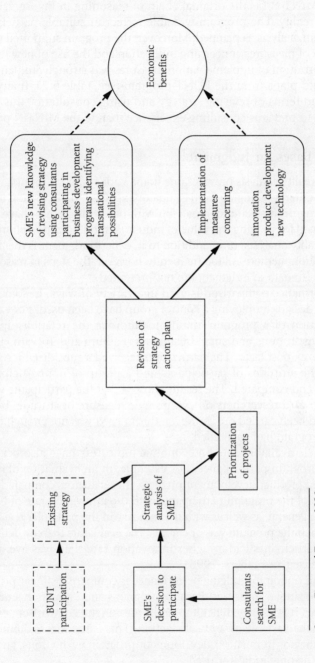

Figure 5.3. Revised Chain of Reasoning for MINT-N, Derived from the Evaluation

Economic benefits

SME's new knowledge
of revising strategy
using consultants
participating in
business development
programs identifying
transnational
possibilities

Implementation of
measures
concerning

innovation
product development
new technology

Revision of
strategy
action plan

Prioritization
of projects

Existing
strategy

Strategic
analysis of
SME

BUNT
participation

SME's
decision to
participate

Consultants
search for
SME

Source: Finne and Torvatn, 1996.

The revised chain of reasoning sums up the main differences between the ideals of MINT-N (as the original chain of reasoning in Figure 5.1) and the observed reality. The program was able to recruit suitable participants and carry out an analysis as planned. Moreover, the program supported the implementation of measures concerning innovation and the use of new technology. The prioritization of implementation measures was strongly influenced, however, by old plans from the BUNT program (see Table 5.2). If any learning occurred in terms of revising strategy and using consultants, this was more likely due to previous consulting experience than to the MINT-N program.

Valuing: Bases for Judgment

The ideal-reality analysis provides one framework and basis for judgment. Several other criteria—ranging from evaluator expertise, participation in a collective learning process, and comparison with other programs—have also been used as bases for judging the value of industrial modernization efforts. As part of ideal-reality analysis, or in addition to it, expert judgment is the most common valuation method. All too frequently, however, the steps in reasoning used to move from data to judgment are not presented.

Performance comparison is used in a variety of ways. In some cases, ex post facto designs employing a control group have been used. For example, in an evaluation of a program aiming to improve the relationship between research institutions and small businesses (Falkum and Torvatn, 1993), the design was ex post facto. The participants received a subsidized research project, and the attitudes of participants and a group of nonparticipants were examined and compared. The results showed that the participants were more positive toward researchers on every single measure of attitude. Because no pretest had been carried out, however, this in itself was not enough to warrant that the program had succeeded.

Publicly available data on economic indicators have also been used to measure program performance. For example, in an evaluation of a program that funded product development projects, the evaluators compared the innovation rate of the program participants with the innovation rate of Norwegian industry in general, as well as with the industry in the particular region of Norway in which the program was operating. The evaluators thereby demonstrated that the participants had a higher innovation rate than was average in the region (Isaksen and others, 1996).

A third option for judging performance is comparing similar programs on the same or similar measures. Because programs and evaluation strategies differ, however, it is usually difficult to find a meaningful comparison, except perhaps with the variable of user satisfaction. This is the most commonly used impact indicator in business development program evaluations, and in some cases it is the only indicator used.

User satisfaction is a poor indicator of program performance, though. In Norway, since the end of the 1980s, almost all evaluations reveal that two-thirds of program participants are satisfied. Yet, we learn little from this finding, for our experience shows few correlations between user satisfaction and other indicators of impact assessment, such as economic success. The main value of user satisfaction is thus as a performance standard; when user satisfaction is low, it can be an important indicator of problems in the program.

In action research evaluations, valuation is conducted in a slightly different way. Although the elements described above (ideal-reality analysis, comparison) might be parts of valuation in an action research evaluation, the valuation process will also include several stakeholders in a joint valuing process. An understanding of the evaluand is cogenerated among evaluators and stakeholders. This learning process is also a valuing process. When the stakeholders understand the evaluand on which they can act, then they also have performed a valuing. In order to take action, the stakeholders must define what is good, what is bad, where there is room for improvement, and so on.

Conclusion

The greatest weakness of Norwegian evaluations in the field of industrial modernization is overreliance on feedback from participants. Participant feedback is a widely used approach (Shapira, Youtie, and Roesner, 1996), and there seems to be little difference between Norway and other nations in that respect. It is efficient in terms of cost and time and provides important data.

The validity of participant feedback as a measure of effect is highly questionable, however. The people who provide this information are strategic actors; they are well aware of the evaluation's purpose and frequently have vested interests in perpetuating the system. In the sole example in which the evaluator had access to data on economic performance in annual reports and asked the companies to provide the same data for an evaluation, the companies overestimated their performance in their report to the evaluator by a factor of two (Rolfsen, 1995).

It is therefore necessary to obtain additional data on performance from other sources. The most accessible source is industrial statistics (including annual reports). Other sources include customer valuation of performance, measures of benchmarks, observed entry into (and retreat from) new markets, observed entry of (and withdrawal from) new products, and establishment of new industrial relations.

Norwegian industrial modernization evaluation also shows several strengths and promising trends. There is a good relationship between evaluators, program shapers, and management, which promotes the use of evaluation. The challenge for the Norwegian evaluation community is to maintain this relationship, while publishing works about the evaluation models employed so that the rest of the evaluation community can learn from these experiences.

Several evaluators have acknowledged the need for program theory. Here, the Norwegian evaluation community faces two tasks. The first is to incorporate the theories that already exist in this area into its practice. The second is to develop the view that some Norwegians hold on program theory—namely, that in any program, there are several program theories, not just one, and that those theories are not static but dynamic; they evolve over time.

Finally, among Norwegian industrial modernization evaluators today, there is a growing awareness of the importance of analyzing the counterfactual. Thus far, additionality analysis has been the method of choice. This method relies on information from one source, however, posing all the validity problems outlined earlier. A more sophisticated counterfactual analysis would require more data from additional sources. Because additionality deals with the most probable use of resources without program participation, a starting point for obtaining more data on this would be the firm's own plans of development at the time of program entry. Another method would be to compare development in participant firms with that in nonparticipant firms. Both of these analyses have already been carried out but only on a limited scale (Finne, 1993). There remains a strong need to develop methods in this area.

References

Arbo, P. *Teknologi og kompetanseorientert støtte. En oversikt over utvalgte tiltak og evalueringer* [Technology and competence-enhancing efforts. An overview of selected efforts and their evaluations]. Tromsø, Norway: Norut Samfunnsforskning, 1993.

Baklien, B. "Evalueringsforskning I Norge" [Evaluation research in Norway]. *Tidsskrift for samfunnsforskning,* 1993, *34* (3), 261–274.

Chen, H.-T. *Theory-Driven Evaluations: A Comprehensive Perspective.* Thousand Oaks, Calif.: Sage, 1990.

Elden, M. "Three Generations of Work Democracy Experiments in Norway." In C. Cooper and E. Mumford (eds.), *The Quality of Working Life in Western and Eastern Europe.* London: Associated Business Press, 1979.

Elden, M., and Levin, M. "Co-Generative Learning: Bringing Participation into Action Research." In W. F. Whyte (ed.), *Participatory Action Research.* Thousand Oaks, Calif.: Sage, 1991.

Elvemo, J., Fossen, Ø., and Levin, M. "Integrating Change Models and Norwegian Experiences: Constructing a Learning-Based Model for Large Systems Change." Paper presented at the conference "From Socialism to Capitalism: The Role of Human Resource Management in Large Systems Change," Gummersbach, Germany, June 1991.

Falkum, E., and Torvatn, H. *For å forske må man kunne forske-en analyse av effekt av DTS-programmet* [To do research you must know how to do research]. Trondheim, Norway: Institute of Social Research in Industry, Foundation for Scientific and Industrial Research, 1993.

Finne, H. *How Does Strategic Planning Influence Technology Strategies in Small Firms?* Trondheim, Norway: Institute of Social Research in Industry, Foundation for Scientific and Industrial Research, 1993.

Finne, H., Levin, M., and Nilssen, T. "Trailing Research: A Model for Useful Program Evaluation." *Evaluation,* 1995, *1* (1), 11–31.

Finne, H., and Torvatn, H. *Evaluation of MINT in Norway.* Trondheim, Norway: Institute of Social Research in Industry, Foundation for Scientific and Industrial Research, 1996.

Guba, E. G., and Lincoln, Y. S. *Effective Evaluation.* San Francisco: Jossey-Bass, 1981.

Guba, E. G., and Lincoln, Y. S. *Fourth Generation Evaluation.* Thousand Oaks, Calif.: Sage, 1989.

Isaksen, A., Karlsen, E. N., Pedersen, T. E., Smith, K., Wiig, H., and Arnold, E. *Evaluering av nyskapnings og teknologiprogrammet for Nord-Norge (NT-programmet)* [Evaluation of the innovation and new technology program for northern Norway (the NT-program)]. Oslo: Studies in Technology, Innovation, and Economic Policy, 1996.

Olsen, J. P. *Norway: Reluctant Reformer, Slow Learner, or Another Triumph of the Tortoise?* Bergen, Norway: LOS-Senteret, 1993.

Patton, M. Q. *Utilization-Focused Evaluation.* (2nd ed.) Thousand Oaks, Calif.: Sage, 1986.

Rolfsen, M. *Evaluering av FRAM programmet. Delrapport C: Analyse av programmets resultater* [Evaluation of the FRAM program. Report C: Impact analysis]. Trondheim, Norway: Institute of Social Research in Industry, Foundation for Scientific and Industrial Research, 1995.

Rush, B., and Ogborne, A. "Program Logic Models: Expanding Their Role and Structure for Program Planning and Evaluation." *Canadian Journal of Program Evaluation,* 1991, 6 (2), 95–106.

Shapira, P. J., and Roesner, J. D. "Evaluating Industrial Modernization: Introduction to the Theme Issue." *Research Policy, 25* (2), 1996, 181–183.

Shapira, P., Youtie, J., and Roesner, J. D. "Current Practices in the Evaluation of US Industrial Modernization Programs." *Research Policy, 25* (2), 1996, 185–214.

Torvatn, H. "Use of Evaluations of Norwegian Technology Transfer Programs." Unpublished doctoral dissertation, Norges Tekniske Høgskole, 1993.

Torvatn, H., and Rønningsbakk, B. *Norske teknologioverføringsprogrammer. Evalueringsmetodikk og resultater-en oppsummering* [Norwegian programs for technology transfer. A summary of results and methods of evaluation]. Trondheim, Norway: Institute of Social Research in Industry, Foundation for Scientific and Industrial Research, 1991.

Trist, E. L. "Evolution of Sociotechnical Systems." In A. H. van de Ven and W. F. Joyce (eds.), *Perspectives on Organization Design and Behavior.* New York: Wiley, 1981.

Weiss, C. H. "Theory-Based Evaluation: Past, Present, and Future." Paper presented at the annual meeting of the American Evaluation Association, Atlanta, Georgia, Nov. 1996.

HANS TORVATN is a researcher at the Institute of Social Research in Industry (IFIM), a division of the Foundation for Scientific and Industrial Research (SINTEF) in Trondheim, Norway.

INDEX

Ordering Information

New Directions for Evaluation is a series of paperback books that presents the latest techniques and procedures for conducting useful evaluation studies of all types of programs. Books in the series are published quarterly in Spring, Summer, Fall, and Winter and are available for purchase by subscription as well as by single copy.

Subscriptions cost $63.00 for individuals (a savings of 28 percent over single-copy prices) and $105.00 for institutions, agencies, and libraries. Please do not send institutional checks for personal subscriptions. Standing orders are accepted. Prices subject to change. (For subscriptions outside of North America, add $7.00 for shipping via surface mail or $25.00 for air mail. Orders must be prepaid in U.S. dollars by check drawn on a U.S. bank or charged to VISA, MasterCard, or American Express.)

Single copies cost $22.00 plus shipping (see below) when payment accompanies order. California, New Jersey, New York, and Washington, D.C., residents please include appropriate sales tax. Canadian residents add GST and any local taxes. Billed orders will be charged shipping and handling. No billed shipments to post office boxes. (Orders from outside North America must be prepaid in U.S. dollars by check drawn on a U.S. bank or charged to VISA, MasterCard, or American Express.)

Shipping (Single Copies Only): $30.00 and under, add $5.50; to $50.00, add $6.50; to $75.00, add $7.50; to $100, add $9.00; to $150.00, add $10.00.

Discounts for quantity orders are available. Please write to the address below for information.

All orders must include either the name of an individual or an official purchase order number. Please submit your order as follows:
  Subscriptions: specify series and year subscription is to begin
  Single copies: include individual title code (such as PE59)

Mail orders to:
  Jossey-Bass Publishers
  350 Sansome Street
  San Francisco, California 94104–1342

Phone subscription or single-copy orders toll-free at (888) 378–2537 or at (415) 433–1767 (toll call).

Fax orders toll-free to: (800) 605–2665.

For subscription sales outside of the United States, contact any international subscription agency or Jossey-Bass directly.

OTHER TITLES AVAILABLE IN THE
NEW DIRECTIONS FOR EVALUATION SERIES
Jennifer C. Greene, Gary T. Henry, Editors-in-Chief

PE76   Progress and Future Directions in Evaluation: Perspectives on Theory, Practice, and Methods, *Debra J. Rog, Deborah Fournier*

PE75   Using Performance Measurement to Improve Public and Nonprofit Programs, *Kathryn E. Newcomer*

PE74   Advances in Mixed-Method Evaluation: The Challenges and Benefits of Integrating Diverse Paradigms, *Jennifer C. Greene, Valerie J. Caracelli*

PE73   Creating Effective Graphs: Solutions for a Variety of Evaluation Data, *Gary T. Henry*

PE72   A User's Guide to Program Templates: A New Tool for Evaluating Program Content, *Mary Ann Scheirer*

PE71   Evaluation and Auditing: Prospects for Convergence, *Carl Wisler*

PE70   Advances in Survey Research, *Marc T. Braverman, Jana Kay Slater*

PE69   Evaluating Initiatives to Integrate Human Services, *Jules M. Marquart, Ellen L. Konrad*

PE68   Reasoning in Evaluation: Inferential Links and Leaps, *Deborah M. Fournier*

PE67   Evaluating Country Development Policies and Programs: New Approaches for a New Agenda, *Robert Picciotto, Ray C. Rist*

PE66   Guiding Principles for Evaluators, *William R. Shadish, Dianna L. Newman, Mary Ann Scheirer, Christopher Wye*

PE65   Emerging Roles of Evaluation in Science Education Reform, *Rita G. O'Sullivan*

PE64   Preventing the Misuse of Evaluation, *Carla J. Stevens, Micah Dial*

PE63   Critically Evaluating the Role of Experiments, *Kendon J. Conrad*

PE62   The Preparation of Professional Evaluators: Issues, Perspectives, and Programs, *James W. Altschuld, Molly Engle*

PE61   The Qualitative-Quantitative Debate: New Perspectives, *Charles S. Reichardt, Sharon E. Rallis*

PE59   Evaluating Chicago School Reform, *Richard P. Niemiec, Herbert J. Walberg*

PE58   Hard-Won Lessons in Program Evaluation, *Michael Scriven*

PE57   Understanding Causes and Generalizing About Them, *Lee B. Sechrest, Anne G. Scott*

PE56   Varieties of Investigative Evaluation, *Nick L. Smith*

PE55   Evaluation in the Federal Government: Changes, Trends, and Opportunities, *Christopher G. Wye, Richard C. Sonnichsen*

PE54   Evaluating Mental Health Services for Children, *Leonard Bickman, Debra J. Rog*

PE53   Minority Issues in Program Evaluation, *Anna-Marie Madison*

PE52   Evaluating Programs for the Homeless, *Debra J. Rog*

PE50   Multisite Evaluations, *Robin S. Turpin, James M. Sinacore*

PE49   Organizations in Transition: Opportunities and Challenges for Evaluation, *Colleen L. Larson, Hallie Preskill*

PE47   Advances in Program Theory, *Leonard Bickman*

PE45   Evaluation and Social Justice: Issues in Public Education, *Kenneth A. Sirotnik*

PE44   Evaluating Training Programs in Business and Industry, *Robert O. Brinkerhoff*

PE43   Evaluating Health Promotion Programs, *Marc T. Braverman*

PE42   International Innovations in Evaluation Methodology, *Ross F. Conner, Michael Hendricks*

PE41   Evaluation and the Federal Decision Maker, *Gerald L. Barkdoll, James B. Bell*

PE40   Evaluating Program Environments, *Kendon J. Conrad, Cynthia Roberts-Gray*

PE39   Evaluation Utilization, *John A. McLaughlin, Larry J. Weber, Robert W. Covert, Robert B. Ingle*